MORE GRUB ON LESS GRANT

Cas Clarke wrote her first book, *Grub on a Grant*, after taking a degree in Urban Studies at Sussex University. She now lives in a rural retreat in Surrey with her husband Andy and children James and Helena.

Also by Cas Clarke

Grub on a Grant
Feast Your Friends
Peckish but Poor
Mean Beans
Posh Nosh
Vegetarian Grub on a Grant
Great Grub for Toddlers

More Grub
On Less Grant

The New Student Cookbook

Cas Clarke

HEADLINE

Copyright © 1999 Cas Clarke

The right of Cas Clarke to be identified as the Author of
the Work has been asserted by her in accordance with the
Copyright, Designs and Patents Act 1988.

First published in 1999
by HEADLINE BOOK PUBLISHING

10 9 8 7 6 5 4 3 2 1

All rights reserved. No part of this publication may be
reproduced, stored in a retrieval system, or transmitted,
in any form or by any means, without the prior written
permission of the publisher, nor be otherwise circulated
in any form of binding or cover other than that in which
it is published and without a similar condition being
imposed on the subsequent purchaser.

Illustrations by Mik Brown

ISBN 0 7472 6171 7

Typeset by
Letterpart Limited, Reigate, Surrey

Printed in England by
Caledonian International Book Manufacturing Ltd, Glasgow

HEADLINE BOOK PUBLISHING
A division of Hodder Headline PLC
338 Euston Road
London NW1 3BH

To Lucy and Sue

Thanks for all the great memories we share!

Contents

Introduction

The original *Grub on a Grant* was written when I finished my course in 1984. This sister book is published in 1999 – in the run-up to the new millennium. During these 15 years there has been a revolution in the way we shop and eat. Superstores are now abundant and it is the prolific growth of such shops that has so altered our way of shopping. I live near Gatwick and have a choice of three of these huge stores and can shop 24 hours a day.

As a family we often holiday in remote parts of the British isles, and superstores have gradually found their way from Land's End to John o' Groats – admittedly more slowly in Scotland, but last time we were in Aviemore Tesco had arrived. In fact, when we go on holiday in Britain I actually pack a small guide to our nearest superstore!

Not only is it more convenient to obtain all your shopping under one roof but with these stores has come a wealth of exotic produce that was never available to us before. The arrival of the new products has certainly changed the British palate and our standard fare has never been so cosmopolitan. All such changes have certainly impacted upon students and what they now eat. Although students have always been big on 'gutsy' flavours such as garlic and curry, these tastes have expanded to cover more exotic flavours. Although curry still features strongly it often now has Thai overtones – one advantage of Thai cooking being that it is often stir-fried which means that the cooking time is shorter and therefore savings can be made on fuel. One particular area that has increased enormously in popularity is the growth of eastern and middle eastern influences. We don't just cook Chinese food now but in a certain style, such as Szechwan or Cantonese.

Japanese food is another noticeable trend, but although I have some wasabi paste in my store cupboard it does not feature in this book for a very good reason.

The most important consideration in student cookery is cost, and the average student cannot afford to have a big store cupboard – which in essence is money just sitting on a shelf. When I started writing this book I wanted to use many different products that I use in my everyday cooking, items which are commonly available in local superstores. However, not many students can afford to keep several different types of soy sauce in their stock cupboard, though when I started this book I had five – light and rich soy sauce, kecap manis (an Indonesian sweet soy sauce), a reduced salt version and kikkomen (Japanese high quality soy). I'd commonly use most of these alongside fish sauce and minced ginger, lemongrass, chilli and garlic just in one dish, and obviously the average student doesn't cook like this.

If you are particularly fond of one style of cooking it might suit you to expand the range of ingredients you keep for that style, but most of us like to vary our menus, so it doesn't pay to stock up on lots of items which take ages to use. So I have kept to simple ingredients that are readily available, and I have also given you tips on other recipes that will use up any items you have bought for a particular recipe and which have a short shelf life. This should keep any wastage to a bare minimum.

Since price is of prime importance I have costed out all these recipes (which was a real eye-opener) and as well as the budget chapter where everything is as cheap as it can be, I have divided the recipes into three types (see page 15).

These costings were current in August 1998 and include the cost of rice, pasta or bread to accompany the meal. The price is per person and where I have stated that the dish will feed for example 4–6 people the costing is based on the lower number, i.e. 4.

Price of course is not the only feature that differentiates student cookery from the norm; when it comes to cooking in halls of residence, there are specific problems with storage and facilities. That is why in this book I have supplied a chapter paying particular attention to these problems.

For all of us life's tempo has increased and most of us spend less time cooking now than we used to. The emphasis nowadays is firmly on food that is quick and easy to prepare and cook and this is certainly reflected here. None of the recipes in this book should take longer than 30 minutes' preparation time and many can actually be prepared and cooked within half an hour.

Traditional British cookery hardly appears in this book at all – not surprising since it is based mainly on meat – as using meat does bump up the cost. There are some recipes based on meat, but the number of vegetarian recipes vastly outweighs the ones using animal proteins. I have also indicated whether the recipe is suitable for vegans.

Stodge used to be part and parcel of the student diet, but nowadays this doesn't suit the student who has been brought up on a more health-conscious diet. Certainly we are much more aware of how our health is affected by what we eat and this has also been reflected here. There is more of an emphasis on fresh produce. This is more readily available now, but if you are stuck on campus and the campus shop's stock has seen better days you would be better off substituting something else or making a different dish entirely.

I have also assumed that you have a bare minimum of culinary skills, that you can actually boil an egg or prepare beans on toast without a guide – although I do know that there are students who can't. (Personally I think their parents should be lined up against a wall and shot!) I have not prepared a guide on snacks. Since an increasing number of students come from families where both parents have worked, you should have got the knack of preparing your own lunch and breakfast by now. And if not you quickly will!

Many students like to get together with friends to produce meals. In *Grub on a Grant* I gave some set menus, shopping lists and time plans. In this book there is one chapter specifically devoted to cooking for eight or more and another for when pooling resources for a Sunday lunch or a special meal to celebrate a birthday or to feed a loved one.

I think that you will find this book invaluable – especially the chapter on simple budget standbys which is your guide to getting through that last week of term when not only your money has gone, but your overdraft too!

Notes on Costings

One sunny day in March 1998 I set off to visit three different superstores and a campus shop. I had with me a list of items which students commonly shop for. The following table shows the results. Not surprisingly the stores had virtually all the items on the list, but it was an eye-opener to find that not only were many of these not even stocked on campus, but the most commonly used foodstuffs such as spaghetti were completely sold out. As you might expect, in most cases the superstores were cheaper than the campus store, the exceptions being potatoes, onions, garlic, egg noodles and cheese.

It was also interesting to find that the campus store had a remarkable stock of Korean food, which was obviously as a result of the influence of foreign students!

When I came to cost out the recipes for this book I visited Sainsbury's again and took a note of all items I had used in the recipes. It was useful to find how prices had changed in a scant six months – some ingredients were more expensive, some were cheaper. I have produced a second table showing how costs differed with the items I had previously checked. Prices are for imperial measures where this was principally how the items were sold.

At the time of writing I have worked out that although it is just possible to feed yourself on £14 a week this can only be done with great difficulty and in practice the diet would be too restrictive over a period of time. I think that most students would need to budget for twice this amount to give them more choice in their diet and to allow for drinks such as coffee, tea or Coke around campus during the day.

By the time this book is published prices no doubt will have altered yet again. But it is useful to have some idea of what things will cost. I am a lot more conscious of prices now and decided to include these price lists for historical interest – you'll be able to look back in years to come and marvel at how cheap some foods were when you were a student!

Product	Tesco Size	Tesco £	Sainsbury's Size	Sainsbury's £	Safeway Size	Safeway £	Campus Size	Campus £
Bag baby spinach	225g	1.69	225g	1.79	225g	1.75	N/A	
Potatoes (12 oz)	.28/lb	0.21 each	.28/lb	0.21 each	.28/lb	0.21 each	.25/lb	0.19 each
Aubergine (9 oz)	.99/lb	0.56 each	.99/lb	0.56 each	.99/lb	0.56 each	1.20/lb	0.68 each
Browncap mushrooms	200g	0.79	250g	0.95	250g	1.15	N/A	
Economy mushrooms	1.19/lb		1.49/lb		3.28/kg		Sold out	
Onion (5–6 oz)	0.29/lb	0.10 each	0.32/lb	0.11 each	.32/lb	0.11 each	0.25/lb	0.08 each
Red pepper		0.69 each	1.09/lb	0.44	1.40/lb	0.70	1.39/lb	0.68
Bulb garlic		0.32 each		0.29 each		0.32 each		0.25 each
Lettuce (2 little gem)		0.79 pack		0.69 pack		0.69 pack	N/A	
Lettuce (round)		0.29 each	Sold out			0.35 each		0.55 each
Spring onions		0.59 bunch		0.59 bunch		0.59 bunch		0.44 bunch
Green chilli	50g pk (3)	0.49	1.89/lb	0.06 each	1.99/lb	0.06 each	2.80/lb	0.09 each
Red chilli	N/A		1.99/lb	0.10 each	N/A		N/A	

Product	Tesco Size	Tesco £	Sainsbury's Size	Sainsbury's £	Safeway Size	Safeway £	Campus Size	Campus £
Coriander (pack)	25g	0.79	15g	0.69	15g	0.69	N/A	
(larger pack)			30g	0.99				
(pot grown)	pot	0.79	pot	0.59	pot	0.79		
Basil (pack)	15g	0.69	15g	0.69	15g	0.69	N/A	
(pot grown)	pot	0.69	pot	0.79	pot	0.79		
Chicken thighs,	8.17/kg		7.61/kg		8.20/kg		N/A	
skinned & boned (pack)	8 × 660g	5.39	4 × 325g	2.49	6 × 482g	3.95		
Minced pork	500g	0.99*	500g	1.49	500g	1.55	N/A	
Frozen stir-fry chicken & veg	312g	1.49	312g	1.49	312g	1.49	312g	1.49
Frozen stir-fry prawns & veg	340g	1.49	340g	1.49	340g	1.49	340g	1.49
Mature Cheddar cheese	2.39/lb		2.39/lb		2..59/lb		3.83/kg	1.72/lb
Natural yogurt	150ml	0.31	150ml	0.35	150ml	0.31	250ml	0.59

* Special offer

Product	Tesco		Sainsbury's		Safeway		Campus	
	Size	£	Size	£	Size	£	Size	£
Double cream	142ml	0.43	5 fl oz	0.43	143ml	0.43	N/A	
Crème fraîche	200g	0.79	200g	0.79	200g	0.79	N/A	
Medium egg noodles	250g	0.69	250g	0.69	250g	0.73	250g	0.68
Spaghetti	Ec 500g	0.19	Ec 500g	0.19	500g	0.35	Sold out	
Pasta (penne or twists)	Ec 500g	0.25	Ec 500g	0.25	500g	0.45	500g	0.52
Tilda basmati rice	1kg	2.49	1kg	2.45	1kg	2.59	N/A	
Risotto rice	500g	1.05	500g	1.65	500g	1.25	N/A	
Berio extra virgin olive oil	500ml	2.99	500ml	2.99	500ml	2.99	250ml	2.09
Own-brand extra virgin olive oil	500ml	2.45	500ml	2.65	500ml	2.69	N/A	
Groundnut oil	1l	1.79	1l	1.79	1l	1.79	N/A	
Sunflower oil	500ml	0.49	500ml	0.49	500ml	0.49	1l	0.89
Vegetable oil	500ml	0.39	500ml	0.39	500ml	0.39	500ml	0.59

Product	Tesco		Sainsbury's		Safeway		Campus	
	Size	£	Size	£	Size	£	Size	£
Soy sauce	150ml	0.56	150ml	0.49	150ml	0.59	Sold out	
Chilli sauce	150ml	0.95	150ml	0.69	150ml	0.99	150ml	0.83
Ginger paste	110g	1.09	110g	1.09	110g	1.09	N/A	
Balti medium curry paste	283g	1.49	283g	1.55	290g	1.49	N/A	
Thai red curry paste	N/A		N/A		200g	1.35	N/A	
Canned coconut milk	400ml	0.72	400ml	0.72	400ml	0.84	400ml	0.89
Madhur Jaffrey curry sauce	350g	1.49	350g	1.49	350g	1.49	N/A	
Cheapest pasta sauce	455g	0.90	400g	1.09	Sold out		500g	1.39
Canned chickpeas	400g	0.45	420g	0.45	420g	0.45	N/A	
Canned flageolet beans	400g	0.49	410g	0.49	400g	0.49	N/A	
Sunflower seeds	100g	0.39	100g	0.39	100g	0.41	N/A	

* Special offer

Product	Sainsbury's March		Sainsbury's August	
	Size	£	Size	£
Bag baby spinach	225g	1.79	225g	1.79
Potatoes (12 oz)	0.28/lb	0.21 each	old pots	N/A
Aubergine (9 oz)	0.99/lb	0.56 each	0.78/lb	0.44 each
Browncap mushrooms	250g	0.95	250g	0.99
Economy mushrooms	1.49/lb		1.28/600g	
Onion (5–6 oz)	0.32/lb	0.11 each	0.29/lb	0.10 each
Red pepper	1.09/lb	0.44	1.49/lb	0.75 each
Bulb garlic		0.29 each		0.25 each
Lettuce (2 Little Gem)		0.69 pack		0.59 pack
Spring onions		0.59 bunch		0.49 bunch
Green chilli	1.89/lb	0.06 each	1.89/lb	0.06 each
Red chilli	1.99/lb	0.10 each	1.99/lb	0.10 each
Coriander (pack)	15g	0.69	15g	0.69
(larger pack)	30g	0.99	30g	0.99
(pot grown)	pot	0.59	pot	0.59
Basil (pack)	15g	0.69	15g	0.69
(pot grown)	pot	0.79	pot	0.79
Chicken thighs,	7.61/kg		7.61/kg	
skinned & boned (pack)	4 × 325g	2.49	4 × 325g	2.49
Minced pork	500g	1.49	500g	2.69
Frozen stir-fry chicken & veg	312g	1.49	312g	1.49
Frozen stir-fry prawns & veg	340g	1.49	340g	1.49
Mature Cheddar cheese	2.69/lb		2.52/lb	
Natural yogurt	150ml	0.35	150g	0.31
Double cream	5 fl oz	0.43	142ml	0.42
Crème fraîche	200g	0.79	200ml	0.79
Medium egg noodles	250g	0.69	250g	0.58
Spaghetti	Ec 500g	0.19	Ec 500g	0.19
Pasta (penne or twists)	Ec 500g	0.25	Ec 500g	0.25

Product	Sainsbury's March		Sainsbury's August	
	Size	£	Size	£
Tilda basmati rice**	1kg	2.45	1kg	2.49
Risotto rice	500g	1.65	500g	1.19
Berio extra virgin olive oil	500ml	2.99	500ml	2.99
Own brand extra virgin olive oil	500ml	2.65	500ml	2.65
Groundnut oil	1l	1.79	1l	1.79
Sunflower oil	500ml	0.49	500ml	0.49
Vegetable oil	500ml	0.39	500ml	0.39
Soy sauce	150ml	0.49	150ml	0.55
Chilli sauce	150ml	0.69	150ml	0.69
Ginger paste	110g	1.09	95g	1.29
Balti medium curry paste	283g	1.55	283g	1.49
Thai red curry paste	N/A		90g	1.49
Canned coconut milk	400ml	0.72	400ml	0.85
Madhur Jaffrey curry sauce	350g	1.49	350g	1.49
Cheapest pasta sauce	400g	1.09	400g	1.09
Canned chickpeas	420g	0.45	420g	0.47
Canned flageolet beans	410g	0.49	410g	0.55
Sunflower seeds	100g	0.39	100g	0.39

** Now selling Economy Basmati for 500g at £1.19

1 Handy Hints

- The measures in all the recipes are approximate, so don't worry if the tin or jar you buy differs slightly from the one that I have used. The only time you need to be more careful is when you are cooking rice or baking. Different types of rice can absorb varying amounts of liquid, so be aware of this and keep an eye on these dishes. If you think the dish is drying out before it is cooked, turn the heat down and/or add a little more liquid.

- Ovens vary enormously. If dishes are coming out overdone, turn the heat down by 10°C/25°F/Gas 1 whenever you cook. Conversely, if dishes always take longer increase the temperature by the same amount.

- Make sure if a recipe says 'gently simmer' that this is what you do, otherwise you could end up with a burnt pan and food. When grilling make sure if cooking fatty meat that you beware of spitting fat or you could end up with a flash fire!

- Quantities of seasonings given are for your guidance only; if you don't like something, omit it or replace it with something else. Alter how much chilli or curry powder you add to suit your own (and your guests') tastes.

- Some recipes use canned beans – to save even more money you can buy them dried, then soak and cook them yourself (if you think the money saved is worth the effort). Use half as many dried beans as the recipe asks for. Soak them overnight, then drain and boil them for 10 minutes (this gets

rid of any toxins in the beans and is essential).
Simmer for 1–1½ hours until the beans are soft.

- If you have half a can of something left over, transfer it to a container – a pudding bowl with a plate over it will do – and keep it in the fridge. If left in the can it may develop a metallic taste.

- It's useful to have a plastic storage box with your name on it to keep items in the fridge. It's also useful to have some clingfilm to wrap half used-up vegetables in – buy the local supermarket's economy version.

- Buy your local supermarket's economy version whenever possible to make huge savings on baked beans, kidney beans, spaghetti, pasta and rice. Although I often specify cans of chopped tomatoes (being extremely lazy myself), it is cheaper if you buy the economy version and chop them yourself. Beware of buying a smaller can that is actually more expensive than the bigger size! You will save money even if you end up wasting half of it.

- Watch out for foodstuffs that have to be kept in the fridge. With fewer preservatives in food many more items, once opened, have to be stored in the fridge and used up within a specified time. You ignore this at your peril, as the dangers of food poisoning are all too real and each year the number of cases goes up.

- In this book, because by nature I am extremely lazy, I have used minced chilli and ginger in many recipes. Where minced chilli has been used you can substitute either ground chilli, dried chilli flakes or a fresh chilli, deseeded and finely chopped. Use whichever is most convenient for you – minced chilli wins hands down for me as the work has been done and the appearance is good when mixed into a dish. Its drawback is that it has to be kept in the fridge and used up within six weeks so if this is a problem for you I would suggest buying either dried chillis which can be crumbled into your cooking or buying them fresh as needs dictate. Minced ginger has the same drawbacks as chilli but is even more convenient to use. However, you can substitute fresh ginger, peeled and grated, or very finely diced. A chunk about 1½ inches (3 cm) long is roughly the same amount as a rounded teaspoonful of minced ginger.

- Symbols used in headings:

£ – Under £1 per serving
££ – Under £1.25 per serving
£££ – Under £1.50 per serving
Prep time – Guidelines on how long it should take to prepare the dish
V – Suitable for vegetarians
Ve – Suitable for vegans
✳ – Can be cooked using only one hob on the cooker

2 The Hairy Hall Experience

What makes cooking conditions so different in halls of residence?

Firstly, facilities are generally not up to much. It is not unknown for 12–20 students to have to share one cooker, so anyone who hogs the cooker is not going to be popular. These recipes are fast and only a couple use the actual oven; most are stir-fried.

Fridge space is also at a premium and the contents of fridges are susceptible to being stolen, so items that have to be refrigerated have been kept to a minimum. Freezers are unknown in most halls – only the ice-box in the fridge is available, so I have used just two products that are bought frozen (and can be bought on campus the day you intend to use them). I have assumed, too, that little money is available for a stock cupboard so such items do not feature heavily.

I know that it can be difficult to buy really fresh vegetables on campus and here have kept mainly to the veggie staples of the student diet, i.e. onions, peppers, tomatoes, mushrooms and carrots. However, even with all these problems it can still be possible to eat well when in hall. In the recipes in this book I have used items such as minced chilli and ginger because of the convenience factor. Since they have to be kept in the fridge and you may have problems with marauding bands of thieves or 'borrowers', all of these items can be bought fresh in small quantities in supermarkets (and sometimes even from campus shops).

These recipes are quick and easy to make and very cosmopolitan in flavour. There are also a few recipes in Chapter 6 that are very well suited to hall life.

If a group of you are going to pool resources it is generally cheaper to use recipes from Chapter 3 rather than double up the quantities here. If you are getting together for a special Sunday lunch you will find suitable recipes in Chapter 5.

Quick Creamy Curry Sauce
Serves 1
Cost: £ Prep time: 15 minutes **V** ✳

Ingredients
　　1 tablespoon (15ml) oil
　　1 onion, chopped
　　2 teaspoons curry powder
　　1 tablespoon (15ml) mango chutney
　　142ml carton double cream

Method
1. Heat the oil and fry the onion until soft and starting to brown.
2. Mix together the rest of the ingredients, then add to the pan.
3. Stir until the sauce thickens slightly.
4. Use to coat cooked vegetables, beans or hard-boiled eggs.

Tip
Serve with some more mango chutney on the side.

Macaroni Magic
Serves 2
Cost: £ Prep and cooking time: 15 minutes **V**

Ingredients
> 1 tablespoon (15ml) oil
> 1 onion, chopped
> 125g quick-cook macaroni
> 330ml ready-made cheese sauce
> 1 teaspoon (5ml) minced chilli or Dijon mustard
> 2 tomatoes, sliced
> 50g cheese, grated

Method
1. Heat the oil and fry the onion until brown.
2. Meanwhile, cook the macaroni in boiling water, according to the packet instructions, then drain.
3. Preheat the grill.
4. Mix together the cheese sauce and chilli or mustard and combine with the macaroni.
5. Place in a heatproof dish and cover with the tomatoes and cheese.
6. Grill until the cheese bubbles and browns.

Tip
Serve with a green salad.

Bean Salsa

Serves 2
Cost: £ Prep time: 5 minutes **V Ve** ✳

Ingredients
> 400g can mixed beans, drained
> 2 tomatoes, chopped
> ½ red pepper, deseeded and finely diced
> ½ bunch of spring onions, sliced
> 1 teaspoon (5 ml) minced chilli
> 1 tablespoon (15ml) oil
> 1 teaspoon (5ml) white wine vinegar
> salt and black pepper

Method
Mix together all the ingredients and season.

Tip
Serve with salad and baked potatoes or rice.

Leftovers

½ red pepper
Red Pepper and Mushroom Kebabs (page 28)
Toasted Omelette Sandwich (page 46)

Spring onions
Chicken Chow Mein (page 33)
Avocado and Salsa Tortillas (page 39)
Thai Lamb (page 52)
Spaghetti Tunagnese (page 163)

Jacket Potato filled with Chilli Beans

Serves 1
Cost: £ Prep time: 5 minutes + cooking time for
potato **V Ve**

Ingredients
    1 large potato

For the filling
    215g can chilli beans

Method
1. Preheat the oven to 220°C/425°F/Gas 7.
2. Prick the potato all over and cook in the preheated oven
   for 1–1½ hours until crispy outside and soft and fluffy
   inside.
3. Meanwhile, prepare your filling.
4. Heat the beans gently in a small saucepan.
5. Cut a large cross in the top of the potato and squeeze to
   open out the potato, then top with the chilli beans.

Tip
Jacket potatoes can also be served with baked, barbecued or
curried beans.

Mushroom Stroganoff
Serves 2
Cost: £ Prep time: 20 minutes **V** ✳

Ingredients
    2 tablespoons (30ml) oil
    1 onion, thinly sliced
    250g chestnut mushrooms, sliced
    1 tablespoon (15ml) whole-grain mustard
    125ml crème fraîche
    salt and black pepper

Method
1. Heat the oil and fry the onion until soft and starting to brown.
2. Add the mushrooms and fry for a few minutes until soft and starting to brown.
3. Stir in the mustard and crème fraîche and just heat through.
4. Season and serve.

Leftovers

Crème fraîche
Tricolor Spaghetti (page 58)
Eggs Florentine (page 165)

Jacket Potatoes filled with Garlic Cheese and Mushrooms
Serves 2
Cost: £ Prep time: 10 minutes + cooking time for
potatoes V

Ingredients
  2 large potatoes

For the filling
  1 tablespoon (15ml) oil
  100g button mushrooms, sliced
  125g soft cheese with garlic
  salt and black pepper

Method
1. Preheat the oven to 220°C/425°F/Gas 7.
2. Prick the potatoes all over and cook in the preheated oven for 1–1½ hours until crispy outside and soft and fluffy inside.
3. Meanwhile, prepare your filling.
4. Heat the oil and fry the mushrooms until soft and starting to brown.
5. Add the cheese and melt down into a sauce, then season.
6. Cut a large cross in the top of each potato and squeeze gently to open out the potato.
7. Top each potato with the filling.

Chinese Omelette Rolls

Serves 2

Cost: £ Prep time: 10 minutes **V** ✳

Ingredients

4 eggs, beaten
4 tablespoons chopped parsley
salt and black pepper
1 tablespoon (15ml) oil
1 carrot, grated
1 courgette, grated
1 tablespoon (15ml) soy sauce
1 tablespoon (15ml) tomato ketchup

Method

1. Beat together the eggs and parsley, then season.
2. Heat the oil and add half the egg mixture.
3. Let the omelette set, drawing back the sides to let any uncooked mixture run underneath. It should only take 2–3 minutes to set.
4. Slide off the pan and repeat with the other omelette.
5. Mix together the remaining ingredients and divide between the two omelettes. Roll up each omelette, then cut in half. Serve immediately.

Tip

You can make these into spicy rolls by adding some minced chilli to the omelette mixture.

Leftovers

2 eggs

Kidney Bean Kedgeree (page 30)
Toasted Omelette Sandwich (page 46)
Pipérade (page 47)
Huevos Rancheros (page 157)
Omelette (page 161)

Dolcelatte-dressed Spaghetti and Leeks
Serves 2
Cost: £ Prep time: 15 minutes **V**

Ingredients
> 175g spaghetti
> 1 tablespoon (15ml) oil
> 1 leek, sliced
> 75g Dolcelatte cheese, diced
> 100g soft cheese
> salt and black pepper

Method
1. Cook the spaghetti in boiling water according to the packet instructions.
2. Heat the oil and fry the leek until soft and starting to brown.
3. Add the cheeses and stir while they blend into a smooth sauce.
4. Drain the spaghetti.
5. Season and stir the sauce into the spaghetti, then serve immediately.

Tip
You can substitute 4 × 21g Dolcelatte portions from the pick 'n' mix selection.

Leftovers

Soft cheese
Tuna-stuffed Jacket Potatoes (page 29)
Soft cheese mixed with grated or chopped celery or chopped spring onions makes a good filling for sandwiches or rolls.

Creamy Courgettes and Walnuts
Serves 2
Cost: **£** Prep time: 10 minutes **V** ✳

Ingredients
2 tablespoons (30ml) oil
2 courgettes, cut into matchsticks
1 celery stick, trimmed and cut into matchsticks
1 onion, chopped
125g soft cheese with garlic
50g walnut pieces
salt and black pepper

Method
1. Heat the oil and fry the vegetables for a few minutes until soft and starting to brown.
2. Add the cheese and melt down into a sauce.
3. Stir in the walnuts, season and serve.

Tip
Serve as a topping for pasta or baked potatoes.

Red Pepper and Mushroom Kebabs
Serves 1
Cost: £ Prep time: 5 minutes + 10 minutes cooking + 1 hour marinating **V Ve** ✳

Ingredients
> ½ red pepper, deseeded and cut into large cubes
> 2 large open mushrooms, quartered
> 2 tablespoons (30ml) soy sauce
> 2 tablespoons (30ml) tomato ketchup

Method
1. Mix together all the ingredients and leave to marinate for 1 hour.
2. Preheat the grill.
3. Thread the pepper and mushroom alternately on to 2 wooden skewers.
4. Grill for 10 minutes, turning once.

Tip
Soak the wooden skewers in water to prevent them burning under the grill.

Leftovers

½ red pepper
Bean Salsa (page 21)
Toasted Omelette Sandwich (page 46)

Tuna-stuffed Jacket Potatoes
Serves 2
Cost: £ Prep time: 15 minutes + cooking time for potatoes

Ingredients
2 baking potatoes
1 tablespoon (15ml) oil
1 small onion, chopped
1 clove garlic, crushed
185g can tuna, drained and broken into chunks
50g soft cheese
salt and black pepper
2 tablespoons grated Cheddar cheese

Method
1. Preheat oven to 200°C/400°F/Gas 6.
2. Prick the potatoes and bake in the preheated oven for 1–1½ hours until cooked through.
3. Meanwhile, heat the oil and fry the onion and garlic until soft and starting to brown at the edges.
4. Remove the potatoes from the oven and preheat the grill.
5. Halve the potatoes and spoon out the flesh.
6. Mix the potato with the onion and garlic, tuna and soft cheese. Season.
7. Place the potato skin shells on a baking dish and stuff with the filling, cover with the grated cheese, then grill until the cheese is melting.

Leftovers

Soft cheese
Dolcelatte-dressed Spaghetti and Leeks (page 26)
Soft cheese mixed with grated or chopped celery or chopped spring onions makes a good filling for sandwiches or rolls.

Kidney Bean Kedgeree

Serves 2
Cost: £ Prep time: 25 minutes **V**

Ingredients
>2 eggs
>1 tablespoon (15ml) oil
>1 onion, chopped
>2 teaspoons curry powder
>125g long-grain rice
>350ml vegetable stock
>400g can red kidney beans, drained
>75ml sour cream
>salt and black pepper
>2 tomatoes, cut into wedges

Method
1. Hard-boil the eggs, then plunge into cold water to cool.
2. Shell the eggs and cut into wedges.
3. Meanwhile, heat the oil and fry the onion until soft.
4. Stir in the curry powder and rice.
5. Add the stock, bring to the boil, then cover and simmer for 10–15 minutes until the rice has cooked.
6. Stir through the kidney beans and sour cream.
7. Season and serve garnished with the eggs and tomatoes.

Leftovers

Sour cream
Avocado and Salsa Tortillas (page 39)

Eggs
Chinese Omelette Rolls (page 25)
Toasted Omelette Sandwich (page 46)
Pipérade (page 47)
Huevos Rancheros (page 157)
Omelette (page 161)

Avocado Salad
Serves 1
Cost: £ Prep time: 5 minutes **V Ve** ✳

Ingredients
> 1 avocado, stoned, peeled and sliced
> 1 little gem lettuce, shredded
> 1½ inch (4cm) piece of cucumber, sliced
> 2 tablespoons (30ml) tomato ketchup
> 1 tablespoon (15ml) soy sauce
> 1 teaspoon (5ml) minced chilli
> 1 heaped tablespoon (25g) sunflower seeds

Method
1. Place the avocado, lettuce and cucumber in a serving bowl.
2. Mix together the tomato ketchup, soy sauce and chilli and use this as a dressing for the salad.
3. Sprinkle with the sunflower seeds.

Tip
Use lettuce and cucumber as a filling for sandwiches – Marmite, lettuce and cucumber is a particularly good combination.

Tomato and Herb Omelette
Serves 1
Cost: **£** Prep time: 5 minutes **V** ✳

Ingredients
>   2 teaspoons (10ml) oil
>   3 eggs, beaten
>   2 tomatoes, roughly chopped
>   salt and black pepper
>   1 tablespoon chopped herbs

Method
1. Heat the oil in a frying pan. Season the eggs and add to the pan.
2. Tip the mixture over the bottom of the pan and draw back the sides to let any uncooked mixture run underneath.
3. Cook for 2–3 minutes until the omelette sets.
4. Add the tomato and herbs, fold over the omelette and slide on to your serving plate.

Tip
Fresh herbs suitable for this are basil, parsley, oregano, tarragon or coriander.

Leftovers

3 eggs
Scrambled Curried Eggs with Chapattis (page 42)
Egg and Lentil Curry (page 50)

Herbs
Baked Tomatoes in Cheesy Cream (page 185)
Roasted New Potatoes (page 187)

Chicken Chow Mein
Serves 2
Cost: £ Prep time: 10 minutes ✳

Ingredients
  - 1 tablespoon (15ml) oil
  - 1 teaspoon (5ml) minced ginger
  - 1 clove garlic, crushed
  - 312g packet frozen chicken chow mein
  - 1 tablespoon (15ml) soy sauce
  - ½ bunch of spring onions, chopped

Method
1. Heat the oil and stir-fry the ginger and garlic for a few seconds before adding the frozen chicken chow mein.
2. Stir-fry for 3–4 minutes before adding the rest of the ingredients.
3. Cook for another 4 minutes before serving.

Tip
Serve with rice.

There is often very little meat to be bought on campus. However, many campus shops have a freezer tucked away which stocks a small range of frozen foods, and this is where you'll find these packets of frozen chicken chow mein.

Leftovers

Spring onions
Bean Salsa (page 21)
Avocado and Salsa Tortillas (page 39)
Thai Lamb (page 52)
Spaghetti Tunagnese (page 163)

Chilli Pizza
Serves 1
Cost: £ Prep time: 15 minutes **V** ✳

Ingredients
> 1 x 150g pizza base
> 2 tablespoons (30ml) tomato purée or ketchup
> 400g can plum tomatoes, drained and chopped
> 50g cheese, grated
> 1 teaspoon (5ml) minced chilli

Method
1. Preheat the oven to 220°C/425°F/Gas 7.
2. Spread the tomato purée or ketchup over the pizza base.
3. Top with the tomatoes and sprinkle with the cheese and chilli.
4. Bake in the preheated oven for 10 minutes until the cheese is bubbling and browning.

Tip
You can make Pizza Margharita by following this recipe but omitting the chilli and adding 1 thinly sliced tomato to the topping.

Undercover Beans
Serves 1
Cost: £ Prep time: 15 minutes + 25 minutes cooking **V**

Ingredients
    1 tablespoon (15ml) oil
    1 onion, chopped
    400g can mixed beans
    330ml curried gravy made with 50g chip shop curry
      gravy granules
    2 slices bread, buttered and cut into triangles

Method
1. Preheat the oven to 180°C/350°F/Gas 4.
2. Heat the oil and fry the onion until starting to brown.
3. Mix in the beans and gravy and transfer to a heatproof dish.
4. Cover with the bread triangles, butter side up.
5. Cook in the preheated oven for 25 minutes.

Chinese Prawns
Serves 2
Cost: £ Prep time: 10 minutes ✳

Ingredients
>340g packet frozen Chinese prawns
>1 teaspoon (5ml) minced ginger
>1 clove garlic, crushed
>2 teaspoons (10ml) Thai red curry paste
>1 tablespoon (15ml) soy sauce

Method
Put all the ingredients in a pan and stir-fry for 5–6 minutes.

Tip
Serve with rice or noodles.

Another useful standby using a frozen dish that can be found in most freezers on campus and in small corner shops.

Leftovers

Thai red curry paste
Thai Crispy Vegetables (page 51)
Spaghethai Bolognese (page 81)
Thai Peanutty Pork (page 97)
Thai Prawn Curry (page 99)

Golden Bean Curry
Serves 1
Cost: £ Prep time: 15 minutes **V** ✳

Ingredients
>   1 tablespoon (15ml) oil
>   1 onion, chopped
>   1 teaspoon paprika
>   400g can black-eyed beans, drained
>   330ml curried gravy made with 50g chip shop curry
>   gravy granules

Method
1. Heat the oil and fry the onion until brown.
2. Add the paprika and beans and stir through.
3. Add the curried gravy and heat through.

Tip
Serve with rice or chapattis.

Garlicky Beans
Serves 1
Cost: £ Prep time: 15 minutes **V** ✳

Ingredients
> 1 tablespoon (15ml) oil
> 1 onion, chopped
> 2 cloves garlic, crushed
> 400g can black-eyed beans, drained
> 40g soft cheese with garlic

Method
1. Heat the oil and fry the onion and garlic until soft and starting to brown.
2. Add the beans and cheese.
3. Stir until the cheese melts into a garlicky sauce.

Tip
Serve with baked potatoes, rice or pasta.

Leftovers

Soft cheese with garlic
Creamed Leek and Courgette Sauce (page 159)
Broccoli Sauce (page 159)
Chickpeas and Veg (page 160)

Avocado and Salsa Tortillas
Serves 2
Cost: £ Prep time: 10 minutes **V** ✳

Ingredients
  1 avocado
  4 tortillas
  ½ bunch of spring onions, chopped
  50g cheese, grated
  75ml sour cream
  2 tablespoons (30ml) hot salsa

Method
1. Peel and remove the stone from the avocado, slice and divide among the tortillas.
2. Sprinkle each tortilla with spring onions and cheese.
3. Spoon the sour cream and hot salsa over the tortillas.
4. Wrap up each tortilla and serve.

Tip
These can be served as a snack or served with salad as a main course.

Bean and Cheese-filled Tortillas can be made by filling tortillas with drained, canned beans and grated cheese.

Leftovers

Sour cream
Kidney Bean Kedgeree (page 30)

Spring onions
Bean Salsa (page 21)
Chicken Chow Mein (page 33)
Thai Lamb (page 52)
Spaghetti tunagnese (page 163)

Croque Monsieur
Serves 1
Cost: £ Prep time: 5 minutes ✳

Ingredients
>   2 thin white bread slices
>   1 teaspoon (5ml) Dijon mustard
>   2 slices Gruyère cheese
>   25g thinly sliced ham
>   butter or margarine, to spread

Method
1. Preheat the grill.
2. Spread one slice of bread with the mustard, top with 1 slice of Gruyère, then pile on the ham.
3. Top with the other Gruyère slice, then the other bread slice.
4. Spread the outside of the sandwich with butter or margarine and grill each side until brown.
5. Cut into two triangles and serve.

Tip
Cheese and ham make a great filling for sandwiches or use to top omelettes or pizzas.

Mexican Bean Soup
Serves 2
Cost: **£** Prep time: 25 minutes **V** ✳

Ingredients
>1 tablespoon (15ml) oil
>1 small onion, chopped
>1 green pepper, deseeded and diced
>400g can chilli beans
>400g can chopped tomatoes
>35g tortilla chips, to serve
>50g cheese, grated, to serve

Method
1. Heat the oil in a small saucepan and fry the onion and pepper for 10 minutes until soft and starting to brown.
2. Add the beans and tomatoes and simmer gently for 10 minutes.
3. Top with the tortilla chips and cheese and serve.

Scrambled Curried Eggs with Chapattis
Serves 1
Cost: **££** Prep time: 5 minutes **V**

Ingredients
>   knob of butter
>   1 teaspoon curry powder
>   3 eggs, beaten
>   2 tablespoons (30ml) milk
>   salt and black pepper
>   2 chapattis

Method
1. Melt the butter in a small saucepan and quickly stir-fry the curry powder for about 20 seconds.
2. Mix together the eggs and milk, season and add to the pan.
3. Stir-fry until the eggs have made a soft set.
4. Meanwhile, heat the chapattis under the grill.
5. Divide the mixture between the chapattis and roll up.

Tip
Serve chapattis instead of rice with curries.

Leftovers

3 eggs
Tomato and Herb Omelette (page 32)
Egg and Lentil Curry (page 50)

Baked Lemon Chicken
Serves 2
Cost: ££ Prep time: 5 minutes + 35 minutes cooking ✳

Ingredients
    4 chicken thighs
    1 tablespoon (15ml) oil
    juice of ½ lemon
    1 tablespoon (15ml) soy sauce
    1 teaspoon sugar

Method
1. Preheat the oven to 190°C/375°F/Gas 5.
2. Put the chicken thighs in a single layer in an ovenproof dish. Spoon over the oil, lemon juice and soy sauce. Sprinkle with the sugar.
3. Cook in the preheated oven for 35 minutes. Serve hot or cold.

Tip
Serve hot with rice or cold with salad.

Zen Walnuts
Serves 1
Cost: **££** Prep time: 10 minutes **V Ve** ✳

Ingredients
>   1 tablespoon (15ml) oil
>   1 onion, chopped
>   100g walnut pieces
>   2 tablespoons demerara sugar
>   1 tablespoon (15ml) soy sauce

Method
1. Heat the oil and fry the onion until starting to brown.
2. Add the walnuts and sugar and cook until the sugar starts to caramelise.
3. Stir in the soy sauce and serve.

Tip
Serve with rice or noodles.

Chilli Vegetables and Noodles
Serves 1
Cost: **££** Prep time: 15 minutes **V Ve ✳**

Ingredients
>   2 tablespoons (30ml) oil
>   1 onion, sliced
>   1 large carrot, peeled and cut into matchsticks
>   100g mushrooms, thickly sliced
>   100g green beans
>   85g packet dried noodles, vegetable flavour
>   1 tablespoon (15ml) minced chilli

Method
1. Heat the oil and fry the onion for 3–4 minutes, then add the other vegetables and stir-fry for 2 minutes.
2. Break up the noodles, then add them to the pan with 200ml boiling water and the contents of the seasoning sachet.
3. Stir well, cover and simmer for 3 minutes.
4. Stir in the chilli and serve.

Tip
Alter the amount of chilli to suit your own taste.

Toasted Omelette Sandwich
Serves 1
Cost: **££** Prep time: 10 minutes **V**

Ingredients
>1 tablespoon (15ml) oil
>1/2 red pepper, deseeded and sliced
>75g mushrooms, sliced
>2 eggs, beaten
>salt and pepper
>2 slices bread
>margarine, to spread

Method
1. Heat the oil and fry the pepper and mushrooms until soft and starting to brown.
2. Season the eggs, add to the pan and cook until the omelette sets.
3. Meanwhile, toast the bread, then spread each slice with margarine.
4. Place the folded omelette on one slice of the toast, then top with the other slice.

Tip
This is great with tomato ketchup.

Leftovers

1/2 red pepper
Bean Salsa (page 21)
Red Pepper and Mushroom Kebabs (page 28)

Eggs
Chinese Omelette Rolls (page 25)
Kidney Bean Kedgeree (page 30)
Pipérade (opposite)
Huevos Rancheros (page 157)
Omelette (page 161)

Pipérade
Serves 2
Cost: **££** Prep time: 20 minutes **V** ✳

Ingredients
> 3 tablespoons (45ml) oil
> 2 onions, thinly sliced
> 1 red pepper, thinly sliced
> 1 green pepper, thinly sliced
> 2 cloves garlic, crushed
> 4 eggs, beaten
> salt and pepper

Method
1. Heat the oil and fry the vegetables with the garlic for a few minutes until softening and starting to brown at the edges.
2. Season the eggs and add to the pan.
3. Cook over a gentle heat, stirring gently to allow the eggs to set.

Tip
This is great served with a green salad and crusty French bread or ciabatta.

You can make this for one person, halve the ingredients and substitute just 1 red pepper for the mixed peppers.

Leftovers

2 eggs
Kidney Bean Kedgeree (page 30)
Toasted Omelette Sandwich (opposite)
Huevos Rancheros (page 157)
Omelette (page 161)

Risotto with Mushrooms and Walnuts
Serves 2
Cost: **££** Prep time: 25 minutes **V Ve ✳**

Ingredients
>   1 tablespoon (15ml) oil
>   1 onion, chopped
>   200g mushrooms, sliced
>   125g risotto rice
>   450ml vegetable stock
>   100g walnuts, broken
>   salt and black pepper

Method
1. Heat the oil and fry the onion until soft.
2. Stir in the mushrooms and rice.
3. Add the stock 150ml at a time and allow this to be absorbed before adding more.
4. When all the stock has been absorbed, stir in the walnuts, season and serve.

Tip
Non-vegans can stir in a little butter just before serving.

Sun-dried Tomato Risotto
Serves 1
Cost: **££** Prep time: 25 minutes **V** ✳

Ingredients
>1 tablespoon (15ml) oil
>1 small onion, chopped
>65g risotto rice
>250ml vegetable stock
>25g Parmesan cheese, grated
>8 sun-dried tomatoes, chopped or sliced
>salt and black pepper

Method
1. Heat the oil and fry the onion until brown.
2. Add the rice and one-third of the stock.
3. Cook until this stock is absorbed, then add half the remaining stock. When this too is absorbed add the remaining stock.
4. When all the stock has been absorbed, stir in the cheese and tomatoes and season.

Tip
Risotto is even better if you stir in a little butter just before serving.

Egg and Lentil Curry
Serves 2
Cost: ££ Prep time: 15 minutes **V**

Ingredients
  3 eggs
  1 tablespoon (15ml) oil
  1 onion, chopped
  2 cloves garlic, crushed
  2 tablespoons medium curry powder
  200ml carton creamed coconut
  400g can brown lentils, drained
  1 tablespoon (15ml) Indian chutney

Method
1. Place the eggs in a saucepan, cover with cold water and bring to the boil.
2. Cook for 10 minutes. Plunge into cold water to cool.
3. Peel off the shells and cut each in half lengthways.
4. Meanwhile, heat the oil and fry the onion and garlic until starting to brown.
5. Add the curry powder and a little creamed coconut and blend into a sauce.
6. Add the rest of the coconut and the lentils.
7. Cook for a few minutes to thicken the sauce.
8. Stir in the chutney and serve the eggs on top of the lentils.

Serve with rice or chapattis.

Leftovers

3 eggs
Tomato and Herb Omelette (page 32)
Scrambled Curried Eggs with Chapattis (page 42)

Thai Crispy Vegetables
Serves 1
Cost: **££** Prep time: 5 minutes **V Ve** ✳

Ingredients
> 2 teaspoons (10ml) Thai red curry paste
> 1 tablespoon (15ml) soy sauce
> 1 teaspoon (5ml) minced lemongrass
> 400g can mixed Oriental vegetables, drained

Method
1. Mix together the curry paste, soy sauce and lemongrass.
2. In a frying pan heat the sauce, then add the vegetables and quickly heat through – do not overcook or they will lose their crunchiness.

Tip
Either buy and finely chop a stem of lemongrass or buy a jar of minced lemongrass if you cook Thai food a lot.

Serve with rice or noodles.

Leftovers

Thai red curry paste
Chinese Prawns (page 36)
Spaghethai Bolognese (page 81)
Thai Peanutty Pork (page 97)
Thai Prawn Curry (page 99)

Thai Lamb
Serves 2
Cost: **£££** Prep time: 25 minutes ✳

Ingredients
1 tablespoon (15ml) oil
1 onion, chopped
2 cloves garlic, crushed
2 teaspoons (10ml) minced ginger
150g lamb neck fillet, thinly sliced
100g mushrooms, sliced
½ bunch of spring onions, sliced
1 teaspoon (5ml) minced chilli
1 tablespoon (15ml) soy sauce
1 teaspoon (5ml) runny honey or demerara sugar

Method
1. Heat the oil and fry the onion, garlic and ginger for 5 minutes.
2. Add the lamb and cook for another 5 minutes.
3. Add the rest of the ingredients and stir-fry for another 2–3 minutes.

Tip
This is really good with rice and more soy sauce for serving.

Leftovers

Spring onions
Bean Salsa (page 21)
Chicken Chow Mein (page 33)
Avocado and Salsa Tortillas (page 39)
Spaghetti Tunagnese (page 163)

Chicken and Banana Creole
Serves 2
Cost: **£££** Prep time: 20 minutes

Ingredients
- 125g long-grain rice
- 330ml chicken stock, made with 1 stock cube and boiling water
- 2 tablespoons (30ml) oil
- 1 medium chicken breast, boned and skinned, cut into strips
- 1 onion, chopped
- 1 clove garlic, crushed
- ½ green pepper, thickly sliced
- 400g can red kidney beans, drained and rinsed
- 1 teaspoon (5ml) minced chilli
- 1 banana, thickly sliced

Method
1. Place the rice in a pan with a tightly fitting lid and cook gently in the stock until all the stock has been absorbed.
2. Meanwhile, heat the oil and fry the chicken, onion, garlic and pepper until soft and starting to brown.
3. Add the beans, cover and cook until soft.
4. Add the remaining ingredients, mix together well and serve.

Tip
Serve with rice.

Leftovers

½ green pepper
Green Curry (page 88)
Coconut Chicken Curry (page 134)

Quick-fix Chicken Noodles
Serves 2
Cost: **£££** Prep time: 15 minutes ✳

Ingredients
> 2 tablespoons (30ml) oil
> 1 onion, sliced
> 1 chicken breast, sliced
> 1 green pepper, deseeded and sliced
> 100g broccoli florets
> 1 teaspoon (5ml) minced ginger (optional)
> 100g packet chow mein flavour dried noodles
> 1 tablespoon (15ml) soy sauce

Method
1. Heat the oil and fry the onion for 3 minutes until starting to brown.
2. Add the chicken and stir-fry for another 3 minutes.
3. Add the pepper, broccoli and ginger (if using), then stir-fry for 2 minutes.
4. Break up the noodles and add them to the pan with 250ml boiling water and the contents of the seasoning packet. Stir, cover and cook for 3–4 minutes or until the water is nearly absorbed.
5. Stir in the soy sauce and serve.

Tip
Serve with rice.

3 Food in a Flash

Once you are living together with some friends, things on the food front certainly improve. Not all students who live in self-catering accommodation are in halls; many are in accommodation with a number of bedrooms which share a living space, kitchen and bathroom. On campus these 'flats' can still be prey to thieves, as many students often do not lock the doors on these communal areas, locking only their own bedrooms. I remember having stuff stolen from the living area (it's all too easy to forget and leave things lying around) and you'll find that even if you have student insurance you are not covered as there was no forced entry.

So remember that if you don't nail down your possessions they will probably walk! These shared accommodations, however, do generally have a more homely feel to them and even though you have not picked the people you are sharing with, it is not uncommon for these to be the very people you will strike up your initial friendships with, then perhaps go on to share accommodation with outside campus. Although most people don't cook and eat together every night, it is usually possible to cook together on some nights and a bonus is that it works out cheaper this way. Cooking and eating together is fun and reflects the big part food plays in our society. Nowadays most people eat out in restaurants fairly regularly, not just on special occasions as was once the norm.

When I was wandering around my old university when doing some research for this book I dropped in at the students union and picked up a uni handbook. In the intros to the union reps more than half of them mentioned food when asked what would be involved in their ideal evening (the same proportion that mentioned alcohol as featuring in their ideal evening!)

So although students may not be able to eat out as often as they would like to, it is possible to share a meal, a few drinks and convivial company.

Jacket Potatoes filled with Avocado and Bacon
Serves 4
Cost: £ Prep time: 10 minutes + cooking time for potatoes

Ingredients
    4 large potatoes

For the filling
    4 rashers bacon, grilled until crispy
    1 avocado, peeled, stoned and cubed
    salt and black pepper

Method
1. Preheat the oven to 220°C/425°F/Gas 7.
2. Prick the potatoes all over and cook in the preheated oven for 1–1½ hours until crispy outside and soft and fluffy inside.
3. Meanwhile, prepare your filling.
4. Crumble or dice the bacon, mix with the avocado, and season.
5. Cut a large cross in the top of each potato and squeeze gently to open out the potato, then top with the filling.

Tricolor Spaghetti
Serves 2
Cost: £ Prep time: 15 minutes **V**

Ingredients
175g spaghetti
50ml crème fraîche
1 clove garlic, crushed
2 sun-dried tomatoes, sliced
fresh basil, shredded
40g Parmesan or other hard cheese, cut into slivers
salt and black pepper

Method
1. Cook the spaghetti in boiling water according to the packet instructions.
2. Meanwhile, mix together the rest of the ingredients except the Parmesan, then season.
3. When the spaghetti is cooked, drain well and return to the pan with the mixed ingredients. Warm through and serve topped with the Parmesan.

Tip
Use a potato peeler to cut fine slivers of cheese for this recipe.

Leftovers

Crème fraîche
Mushroom Stroganoff (page 23)
Eggs Florentine (page 165)

Gado Gado Salad

Serves 4

Cost: **£** Prep time: 15 minutes **V**

Ingredients

For the salad
    4 eggs
    1 iceberg lettuce, finely shredded
    2 carrots, peeled and cut into fine shavings
    ½ cucumber, peeled and cut into matchsticks

For the peanut dressing
    4 tablespoons crunchy peanut butter
    juice of 1 lime
    1 dessertspoon (10ml) honey or sugar
    1 tablespoon (15ml) soy sauce
    ½ teaspoon (2.5ml) minced chilli

Method
1. Place the eggs in cold water and bring to the boil.
2. Cook for 10 minutes, then plunge into cold water to cool.
3. Shell the eggs and cut each in half lengthways.
4. Place the salad ingredients in a bowl.
5. Put all the peanut dressing ingredients in a pan and heat gently, stirring until they combine.
6. Drizzle the dressing over the salad and serve immediately.

Leftovers

2 eggs
Toasted Omelette Sandwich (page 46)
Huevos Rancheros (page 157)

Spaghetti Putanesca

Serves 4
Cost: £ Prep time: 15 minutes

Ingredients
    450g spaghetti
    2 tablespoons (30ml) oil
    1 onion, chopped
    2 cloves garlic, crushed
    1 tablespoon capers
    220g can chopped tomatoes
    100g stoned black olives
    50g can anchovies in oil, drained

Method
1. Cook the spaghetti in boiling water according to the packet instructions.
2. Heat the oil and fry the onion and garlic for a few minutes until starting to brown.
3. Add the remaining ingredients, cover tightly and simmer for 10 minutes.
4. When the spaghetti is cooked, drain and serve topped with the sauce.

Tip
This is a very gutsy sauce. If the flavours are too strong for you, try cooking it without the anchovies and adding the olives just before serving.

Sausage and Bean Casserole
Serves 4
Cost: **£** Prep time: 5 minutes + 15 minutes cooking

Ingredients
- 2 tablespoons (30ml) oil
- 16 small sausages
- 2 cloves garlic, crushed
- 400g can chopped tomatoes
- 400g can baked beans
- 400g can mixed beans, drained
- ½ teaspoon dried thyme
- 200ml chicken or vegetable stock, made with 1 stock cube and boiling water
- black pepper

Method
1. Heat the oil and fry the sausages until brown all over.
2. Put the sausages and all the remaining ingredients in a large saucepan and season.
3. Bring to the boil, cover tightly and simmer for 20 minutes.

Tip
This is very good served with garlic bread and salad.

Jacket Potatoes filled with Onions and Sausages
Serves 4
Cost: £ Prep time: 30 minutes + cooking time for potatoes

Ingredients
 4 large potatoes

For the filling
 1 tablespoon (15ml) oil
 4 sausages
 1 onion, sliced
 2 tablespoons (30ml) whole-grain mustard

Method
1. Preheat the oven to 220°C/425°F/Gas 7.
2. Prick the potatoes all over and cook in the preheated oven for 1–1½ hours until crispy outside and soft and fluffy inside.
3. Meanwhile, prepare your filling.
4. Heat the oil and fry the sausages for about 20 minutes until browned all over and cooked inside.
5. Remove from the pan and cut each sausage into large chunks.
6. Add the onion to the pan and fry until brown, then return the sausages to the pan and stir in the mustard.
7. Cut a large cross in the top of each potato and squeeze gently to open out the potato, then top with the onions and sausages.

Cabanos Sausage and Pepper Sauce
(for pasta)
Serves 4
Cost: £ Prep time: 20 minutes ✳

Ingredients
    2 tablespoons (30ml) oil
    1 onion, sliced
    3 peppers of mixed colours, deseeded and sliced
    2 cloves garlic, crushed
    400g can chopped tomatoes
    1 teaspoon dried oregano
    2 cabanos sausages, peeled and cut into chunks
    salt and black pepper

Method
1. Heat the oil and fry the onion, peppers and garlic until softened.
2. Add the tomatoes, oregano and sausages, season and cook for 5 minutes to thicken the sauce before serving.

Lamb Korma
Serves 4
Cost: £ Prep time: 15 minutes + 20 minutes cooking ✳

Ingredients
> 1 tablespoon (15ml) oil
> 1 large onion, chopped
> 2 cloves garlic, crushed
> 225g baking potato, peeled and diced
> 500g minced lamb
> 1 tablespoon korma curry powder
> 200ml boiling water
> 2 tablespoons (30ml) Indian chutney
> salt and pepper

Method
1. Heat the oil and fry the onion and garlic for 5 minutes until soft and starting to brown.
2. Add the potato and lamb and stir-fry for 5 minutes until the meat has browned.
3. Add the rest of the ingredients and season.
4. Bring to the boil, cover tightly and simmer for 20 minutes.

Stuffed Pitta Breads
Serves 4
Cost: £ Prep time: 10 minutes **V** ✳

Ingredients
    400g can chickpeas, drained
    4 inch (10cm) piece cucumber, diced
    1 avocado, stoned, peeled and diced
    4 spring onions, sliced
    Peanut Butter Sauce (page 179)
    6 pitta breads

Method
1. Mix together the chickpeas, cucumber, avocado and spring onions and dress with the peanut butter sauce.
2. Grill the pitta breads until they swell, then cut each in half.
3. Stuff each pitta bread with the chickpea mixture and serve.

Tortilla-topped Mexican Pie

Serves 4
Cost: £ Prep time: 15 minutes + 25 minutes cooking

Ingredients
> 2 tablespoons (30ml) oil
> 1 leek, sliced
> 2 cloves garlic, crushed
> 2 carrots, diced
> 250g minced beef
> 1 teaspoon (5ml) minced chilli
> 300ml thick beef gravy, made with 30g gravy granules
>   and boiling water
> 400g can red kidney beans, drained and rinsed
> 30g packet tortilla chips
> 25g cheese, grated

Method
1. Preheat the oven to 200°C/400°F/Gas 6.
2. Heat the oil and fry the leek, garlic and carrots until softened.
3. Add the beef and chilli and cook for a further 5 minutes to brown the meat.
4. Add the gravy and beans, mix well and place in an ovenproof dish.
5. Cover with the tortillas and sprinkle with the cheese.
6. Bake in the preheated oven for 25 minutes.

Cauliflower, Chickpea and Tomato Curry
Serves 4
Cost: **£** Prep time: 10 minutes + 25 minutes
cooking **V Ve** ✳

Ingredients
>   1 tablespoon (15ml) oil
>   1 large onion, chopped
>   2 cloves garlic, crushed
>   4 tablespoons (60ml) medium balti curry paste
>   1 small cauliflower, divided into florets
>   375ml vegetable stock, made with 1 stock cube and
>   boiling water
>   4 tomatoes, cut into wedges
>   400g can chickpeas, drained
>   2 tablespoons (30ml) Indian chutney
>   salt and black pepper

Method
1. Heat the oil and fry the onion and garlic until starting to brown.
2. Stir in the curry paste, add the cauliflower and stock and bring to the boil, then cover tightly and simmer for 15 minutes.
3. Add the tomatoes, chickpeas and chutney and continue to cook, uncovered, for 10 minutes.
4. Season and serve.

Tip
If finances allow it, chopped coriander can be added to the finished dish.

Ham, Mushroom and Basil Sauce
(for pasta)
Serves 4
Cost: £ Prep time: 15 minutes ✱

Ingredients
50g butter
2 tablespoons (30ml) olive oil
250g button or chestnut mushrooms, thinly sliced
100g ham, diced
4 tablespoons chopped fresh basil
salt and black pepper

Method
1. Heat the butter and oil and fry the mushrooms until soft and starting to brown.
2. Add the ham and basil, season and serve.

Tip
Tagliatelle is very good with this sauce.

Farfalle with Pepperoni and Olives

Serves 4

Cost: £ Prep time: 15 minutes

Ingredients
> 400g farfalle pasta
> 2 tablespoons (30ml) oil
> 2 onions, chopped
> 2 cloves garlic, crushed
> 1 teaspoon (5ml) minced chilli
> 400g can chopped tomatoes
> 100g pepperoni, roughly chopped
> 50g stoned black olives

Method
1. Cook the farfalle in plenty of boiling water according to the packet instructions.
2. Meanwhile, heat the oil and fry the onions and garlic until soft and starting to brown.
3. Add the chilli and tomatoes and simmer, uncovered, for 5 minutes.
4. When the pasta is cooked, drain and divide between 4 serving bowls.
5. Stir the pepperoni and olives into the sauce and spoon over the pasta.

Sweetcorn and Mixed Bean Salad
Serves 4
Cost: **£** Prep time: 5 minutes **V** ✳

Ingredients

For the salad
 300g can sweetcorn, drained
 400g can butter beans, drained
 300g can broad beans, drained
 3 celery sticks, sliced
 1 bunch of spring onions, sliced

For the dressing
 2 tablespoons (30ml) oil
 1 tablespoon (15ml) lemon juice
 1 clove garlic
 salt and black pepper
 150g carton natural yogurt

Method
1. Mix together the salad ingredients in a shallow serving dish.
2. Whisk together the oil, lemon juice and garlic and combine with the beans.
3. Season, then drizzle with the yogurt.

Bobotie
Serves 4
Cost: £ Prep time: 15 minutes + 40 minutes cooking

Ingredients
> 1 tablespoon (15ml) oil
> 1 onion, chopped
> 2 cloves garlic, crushed
> 1 tablespoon (15ml) medium balti curry paste
> 500g minced beef
> 2 tablespoons (30ml) tomato purée
> 1 tablespoon (15ml) white wine vinegar
> 50g sultanas
> 2 tablespoons (30ml) mango chutney
> 1 slice bread soaked in 3 tablespoons (45ml) milk, mashed
> 1 banana, mashed
> salt and pepper
> 2 eggs, beaten
> 200ml milk

Method
1. Preheat the oven to 180°C/350°F/Gas 4.
2. Heat the oil and fry the onion and garlic until starting to brown.
3. Add the curry paste and beef and stir-fry until browned.
4. Add the tomato purée, vinegar, sultanas, chutney, mashed bread and banana.
5. Season and transfer to an ovenproof dish.
6. Mix together the eggs and milk, season and pour over the meat mixture.
7. Bake in the preheated oven for 40 minutes or until the egg mixture has set.

Leftovers

Eggs
Chinese Omelette Rolls (page 25)
Kidney Bean Kedgeree (page 30)
Toasted Omelette Sandwich (page 46)
Pipérade (page 47)
Omelette (page 161)

Vegetable Bake

Serves 4
Cost: £ Prep time: 30 minutes + 40 minutes
cooking **V Ve**

Ingredients
    1 aubergine
    3 tablespoons (45ml) olive oil
    4 onions, sliced
    2 cloves garlic, crushed
    200g mushrooms, sliced
    sprinkling of dried thyme
    salt and pepper
    8 tomatoes
    2 courgettes

Method
1. Preheat the oven to 180°C/350°F/Gas 4.
2. Prick the aubergine all over with a fork and place in a roasting tin. Bake in the preheated oven for 25 minutes, then leave to cool.
3. Meanwhile, heat 2 tablespoons (30ml) of the oil and fry the onions and garlic for 5–10 minutes until softened and starting to brown.
4. Add the mushrooms and stir-fry for a further 2 minutes until starting to soften.
5. Place the onion and mushroom mixture in an ovenproof dish. Skin the aubergine and cube the soft flesh, then stir into the dish. Sprinkle with thyme and season.
6. Slice the tomatoes and courgettes to provide enough slices to arrange them alternately on top of the onion mixture.
7. Season again, drizzle with the remaining oil and bake in the preheated oven for 30–40 minutes until cooked through and the courgettes and tomatoes are starting to brown at the edges.

Tip
As well as being a good vegetarian or vegan main dish this can also be used as a vegetable dish when serving meat, and makes a good addition to a party buffet.

Pasta Pie
Serves 4–6
Cost: £ Prep time: 10 minutes + 25–30 minutes cooking **V**

Ingredients
    1 tablespoon (15ml) oil
    450g leeks, sliced
    1 clove garlic, crushed
    4 eggs, beaten
    142ml carton single cream
    125g Gruyère cheese, grated
    125g cooked pasta, roughly chopped
    salt and black pepper

Method
1. Preheat the oven to 180°C/350°F/Gas 4.
2. Heat the oil and fry the leeks and garlic until soft and starting to brown.
3. Mix the leeks and garlic with all the remaining ingredients, season and place in a greased ovenproof dish or tin.
4. Bake in the preheated oven for 25–30 minutes until the eggs have set and the top is a golden brown colour.
5. Serve hot or cold in wedges.

Rice Medley
Serves 4
Cost: £ Prep time: 25 minutes ✳

Ingredients
>   2 tablespoons (30ml) oil
>   1 onion, chopped
>   1 red pepper, deseeded and diced
>   1 clove garlic, crushed
>   250g long-grain rice
>   700ml chicken stock
>   salt and black pepper
>   300g can sweetcorn, drained
>   1 bunch of spring onions, chopped
>   185g can tuna in spring water, drained

Method
1. Heat the oil and fry the onion, pepper and garlic until soft and starting to brown.
2. Stir in the rice, then add the stock. Season and cook, stirring occasionally, until the rice is cooked and has absorbed the stock – about 10–15 minutes.
3. Stir in the rest of the ingredients and serve.

Tip
We like this served with either a sweet chilli sauce or smoky barbecue sauce.

Lamb Kebabs
Serves 4
Cost: £ Prep time: 15 minutes ✳

Ingredients
> 500g minced lamb
> 2 teaspoons curry powder
> salt and pepper

Method
1. Preheat the grill
2. Mix together the lamb and curry powder, then season.
3. Shape into little sausages and thread on to wooden skewers.
4. Cook under the preheated grill for 10 minutes, turning once.

Tip
1 tablespoon chopped mint can be mixed into the kebab mixture. This adds to the flavour, but it's not worth buying mint specifically for this dish.

Bean and Yogurt Salad
Serves 4
Cost: **£** Prep time: 20 minutes + cooling **V** ❄

Ingredients
    2 tablespoons (30ml) oil
    1 onion, chopped
    1 clove garlic, crushed
    1 red pepper, deseeded and cubed
    1 yellow pepper, deseeded and cubed
    2 courgettes, sliced
    4 tomatoes, cut into wedges
    400g can flageolet beans, drained and rinsed
    1 heaped tablespoon raisins
    150g carton natural yogurt

Method
1. Heat the oil and fry the onion and garlic for a few minutes until starting to soften.
2. Add the peppers and courgettes and cook for a further 5 minutes.
3. Add the tomatoes, beans and raisins, and cook gently just to get the tomato juices running.
4. Allow to cool, then top with the yogurt and serve.

Tip
You can also make this substituting sour cream for the natural yogurt.

Mushroom-stuffed Filo Pie

Serves 4
Cost: £ Prep time: 20 minutes + 20 minutes
cooking **V Ve**

Ingredients
2 tablespoons (30ml) oil
1 onion, chopped
2 cloves garlic, crushed
250g chestnut mushrooms, sliced
250g button mushrooms, halved
1 tablespoon (15ml) soy sauce
300ml gravy made with 30g vegetarian gravy granules
black pepper
4 sheets filo pastry
melted butter

Method
1. Preheat the oven to 180°C/350°F/Gas 4.
2. Heat the oil and fry the onion and garlic until starting to brown, then add both types of mushroom and stir-fry until soft.
3. Stir in the soy sauce and gravy, season and transfer to an ovenproof dish.
4. Cover with the sheets of filo, brushing each one with melted butter. Arrange them so they overlap, crumpling each sheet at the edges and tucking into the dish.
5. Brush the finished dish with butter and bake in the preheated oven for 15–20 minutes until golden brown.

Tip
Freeze the rest of the pastry for another pie or use to make Feta-filled Filo (page 84).

Chilli, Tomato and Spinach Sauce
(for pasta)
Serves 4
Cost: £ Prep time: 15 minutes **V Ve** ✳

Ingredients
> 12 sun-dried tomatoes, and 2 tablespoons (30ml) of
>   the oil from the jar
> 2 cloves garlic, crushed
> 1 teaspoon (5ml) minced chilli
> 690g jar passata (sieved tomatoes)
> 225g fresh baby spinach

Method
1. Roughly chop the sun-dried tomatoes and fry in the oil
   with the garlic and chilli for 1 minute.
2. Add the passata and simmer for 5 minutes.
3. Add the spinach and cook until wilted.
4. Serve poured over your favourite pasta.

Leftovers

Sun-dried tomatoes
Tricolor Spaghetti (page 58)
Vegetarian Pasta Bake (page 146)

Cheese and Nut Risotto
Serves 4
Cost: £ Prep time: 25 minutes **V** ✳

Ingredients
> 2 tablespoons (60ml) oil
> 1 large onion, chopped
> 2 cloves garlic, crushed
> 250g risotto rice
> 1 teaspoon thyme
> 900ml vegetable stock, made with 2 stock cubes and
>   boiling water
> 100g Parmesan cheese, finely grated
> 100g walnut pieces
> salt and black pepper

Method
1. Heat the oil and fry the onion and garlic until soft and starting to brown.
2. Add the rice and stir through to coat with oil.
3. Add the thyme and one-third of the stock.
4. Cook until that stock is absorbed, then add half the remaining stock.
5. When that is absorbed add the last of the stock.
6. When all the stock has been absorbed, stir in the Parmesan and walnuts, season and serve.

Hasta Arriba Salad
Serves 4
Cost: £ Prep time: 10 minutes ✳

Ingredients
> 1 tablespoon (15ml) oil
> 500g minced beef
> 2 cloves garlic, crushed
> 1 tablespoon (15ml) tomato purée
> 2 teaspoons (10ml) minced chilli
> 400g can red kidney beans, drained and rinsed
> 2 tablespoons (30ml) salsa
> salt and black pepper

For the salad
> lettuce leaves, shredded
> ½ cucumber, halved lengthways and sliced
> 2 tomatoes, cut into wedges
> 35g packet tortilla chips

Method
1. Heat the oil and fry the beef and garlic for 5 minutes until the meat has browned.
2. Stir in the tomato purée.
3. Add the chilli, kidney beans and salsa, season and stir-fry for a few minutes to heat through.
4. Meanwhile, mix together the salad ingredients and divide between 4 bowls.
5. Mix the hot mince into the salad and serve.

Tip
This is great served with crusty bread and some grated cheese and sour cream.

Leftovers

Salsa
Avocado and Salsa Tortillas (page 39)

Spaghethai Bolognese
Serves 4
Cost: £ Prep time: 25 minutes

Ingredients
75–100g spaghetti per person
1 tablespoon (15ml) oil
500g minced pork
1 teaspoon (5ml) minced ginger
1 teaspoon (5ml) minced lemongrass
2 cloves garlic, crushed
1 tablespoon (15ml) Thai red curry paste
1 tablespoon (15ml) tomato purée
1 tablespoon (15ml) soy sauce
2 tablespoons chopped spring onions
a few basil leaves, roughly torn (optional)

Method
1. Cook the spaghetti in plenty of boiling water according to the packet instructions.
2. Heat the oil and fry the pork for 5 minutes, stirring to break up any lumps.
3. Add all the remaining ingredients except the spring onions and basil. Stir well and cook for another 5 minutes.
4. Add the spring onions and 200ml water. Simmer for 5 minutes.
5. When the spaghetti is cooked, drain and place in serving bowls.
6. Stir the basil into the sauce and spoon over the spaghetti. Serve.

Tip
This is a very versatile recipe which could even stretch to 6 servings if you served it with more spaghetti. Either finely chop a stem of lemongrass for this recipe or buy some minced lemongrass if you cook a lot of Thai food.

Risi e Bisi
Serves 4
Cost: £ Prep time: 25 minutes ✳

Ingredients
    1 tablespoon (15ml) olive oil
    1 tablespoon (15ml) butter
    1 onion, chopped
    2 cloves garlic, crushed
    250g risotto rice
    900ml chicken stock, made with 1 stock cube and
        boiling water
    450g peas
    25g Parmesan cheese, grated
    100g ham, finely chopped
    1 bunch of parsley, finely chopped
    salt and black pepper

Method
1. Heat the oil and butter and fry the onion and garlic until starting to brown.
2. Add the rice, give a quick stir, then add 300ml of the stock.
3. Cook until that stock is absorbed, then add another 300ml stock.
4. When that is absorbed add the rest of the stock and the peas.
5. When the stock is nearly absorbed the rice should be cooked. Stir in the Parmesan, ham and parsley, season and serve immediately.

Tuna and Roasted Vegetable Salad
Serves 4
Cost: **££** Prep time: 5 minutes + 35 minutes cooking + cooling ✳

Ingredients
> 1 aubergine, cut into chunks
> 2 red peppers, deseeded and sliced
> 2 red onions, peeled and quartered
> 1 clove garlic, crushed
> 4 tablespoons (60ml) olive oil
> pinch of oregano
> salt and black pepper
> 185g can tuna, drained and flaked
> 100g stoned black olives

Method
1. Preheat the oven to 220°C/425°F/Gas 7.
2. Mix the aubergine, peppers, onions and garlic with the oil and oregano and season.
3. Place on a baking tray and roast in the preheated oven for 30–35 minutes until the vegetables are starting to blacken at the edges.
4. Leave to cool, then serve the vegetables topped with the tuna and olives.

Feta-filled Filo

Serves 4

Cost: **££** Prep time: 15 minutes + 15 minutes cooking **V** ✳

Ingredients
> 12 sheets filo pastry
> melted butter

For the filling
> 200g feta cheese, crumbled
> 100g Gruyère cheese, grated
> 2 eggs, beaten
> salt and pepper

Method
1. Preheat the oven to 180°C/350°F/Gas 4.
2. Mix together the filling ingredients.
3. Brush a filo sheet with melted butter. Place some filling in the middle and bottom of the sheet of pastry, fold each side inwards, then roll the sheet up. (It should look like a Chinese spring roll.)
4. Brush with more butter and put on a baking tray.
5. Repeat with the other filo sheets.
6. Bake in the preheated oven for 15 minutes until light brown in colour. Serve hot or cold.

Tip
These are great served with garlic bread and salad.

Pork Chilli

Serves 4

Cost: **££** Prep time: 15 minutes + 20 minutes cooking ✳

Ingredients
- 1 tablespoon (15ml) oil
- 1 large onion, chopped
- 2 cloves garlic, crushed
- 1 green pepper, deseeded and diced
- 450g minced pork
- 1 tablespoon (15ml) minced chilli
- 1 teaspoon oregano
- 500g carton passata (sieved tomatoes)
- 400g can red kidney beans, drained and rinsed

Method
1. Heat the oil and fry the onion, garlic and pepper for 5–10 minutes until soft and starting to brown.
2. Add the pork and stir-fry for another 5 minutes to brown the meat.
3. Add the rest of the ingredients, bring to the boil, cover and simmer for 20 minutes.

Tip
This can be served with rice, pasta or baked potatoes.

Greek Feta and Vegetable Casserole
Serves 4
Cost: **££** Prep time: 15 minutes + 15 minutes cooking **V**

Ingredients
> 4 tablespoons (60ml) olive oil
> 1 large onion, thinly sliced into rings
> 3 peppers of mixed colours, deseeded and cut into
> rings
> 4 cloves garlic, crushed
> 4 tomatoes, chopped
> 200g feta cheese, cubed
> 1 teaspoon oregano
> black pepper

Method
1. Preheat the oven to 200°C/400°F/Gas 6.
2. Heat 3 tablespoons (45ml) of the oil and fry the onion, peppers and garlic until soft and starting to brown.
3. Add the tomatoes and cook for a few more minutes to soften.
4. Transfer to an ovenproof dish and mix in the feta and oregano.
5. Season, drizzle with remaining oil, cover tightly, then bake in the preheated oven for 15 minutes.

Tandoori Chicken
Serves 4
Cost: **££** Prep time: 35 minutes ✳

Ingredients
> 8 chicken drumsticks
> 8 chicken thighs
> 1 tablespoon tikka spice powder
> 2 cloves garlic, crushed
> 1 tablespoon (15ml) tomato purée
> 1 tablespoon (15ml) lemon juice
> 75ml sour cream
> salt and pepper

Method
1. Preheat the oven to its highest temperature.
2. Make deep slashes all over the chicken pieces.
3. Mix together all the rest of the ingredients in a bowl, then add the chicken and cover with the mixture. If you have time, cover and leave in the fridge for a while to marinate, or transfer to an ovenproof dish and cook in the preheated oven for 35 minutes until well cooked and blackening.

Tip
These are lovely served with lemon wedges, tomato and onion slices and a crisp green salad. Mint or Cucumber Raita (page 178) also goes well with them.

Leftovers

Sour cream
Kidney Bean Kedgeree (page 30)
Avocado and Salsa Tortillas (page 39)

Green Curry
Serves 2
Cost: **££** Prep time: 25 minutes **V** ✳

Ingredients
2 tablespoons (30ml) oil
1 onion, chopped
½ green pepper, deseeded and cubed
2 cloves garlic, crushed
1 teaspoon (5ml) minced ginger
100g green beans, halved
100g broccoli, divided into small florets
100g peas
1 tablespoon medium curry powder
1 tablespoon (15ml) water
142ml carton double cream
15g pack coriander, chopped

Method
1. Heat the oil and fry the onion, pepper, garlic and ginger until soft and starting to brown.
2. Add the rest of the vegetables and stir-fry for 5 minutes.
3. Whisk together all the remaining ingredients and add to the curry.
4. Heat gently until the sauce thickens slightly.

Tip
This is a good recipe for using up bits and pieces of leftover vegetables.

Leftovers

½ green pepper
Chicken and Banana Creole (page 53)
Coconut Chicken Curry (page 134)

Dhal and Spinach Curry
Serves 2
Cost: **££** Prep time: 20 minutes **V Ve** ✳

Ingredients
1 tablespoon (15ml) oil
1 onion, chopped
1 clove garlic, crushed
1 teaspoon (5ml) minced ginger
1 teaspoon (5ml) minced chilli
2 tablespoons (30ml) medium balti curry paste
220g can chopped tomatoes
225g fresh or frozen spinach
400g can lentil dhal

Method
1. Heat the oil and fry the onion and garlic until starting to brown.
2. Stir in the rest of the ingredients.
3. When the spinach has wilted into the curry and the curry is hot, serve.

Lebanese Bake
Serves 2
Cost: **££** Prep time: 15 minutes + 1 hour cooking

Ingredients
250g baby aubergines
1 tablespoon (15ml) olive oil
1 onion, finely diced
250g minced beef
½ teaspoon each of minced ginger, cinnamon and cumin
1 tablespoon curry powder
125ml water
1 tablespoon raisins
3 tomatoes
few leaves of mint, chopped (optional)

Method
1. Preheat the oven to 200°C/400°F/Gas 6.
2. Cut the stalk end off each baby aubergine and lay them, cut side upwards, in an ovenproof dish or roasting tin.
3. Heat the oil and fry the onion for a few minutes until starting to brown.
4. Add the beef and stir-fry quickly, breaking up any lumps. Add the spices, curry powder, water and raisins, stir well and cook for a few minutes.
5. Spoon the meat sauce over the baby aubergines, then cut the tomatoes into thick slices (about 3 or 4 from each tomato) and surround the aubergines with these. Sprinkle with the mint (if using).
6. Cover the dish with roasting foil or a tight-fitting lid and cook for 50–60 minutes, until the aubergine is well cooked and soft.

Tip
Serve with rice or pitta bread and Cucumber or Mint Raita (page 178). If you can't get baby aubergines (usually from Asian grocers) use 2 larger aubergines and, after halving them, prick them all over to help them cook through.

For a veggie version of this dish substitute 200g finely chopped mushrooms for the minced meat and add some more oil when frying.

Parsley Pesto
Serves 1
Cost: **££** Prep time: 10 minutes **V** ✳

Ingredients
    15g pack parsley, chopped
    2 tablespoons Parmesan cheese, finely grated
    2 tablespoons finely chopped walnuts
    2 teaspoons (10ml) oil

Method
Mix together all the ingredients. Serve as a topping for your favourite pasta.

Tip
You can substitute finely chopped pine nuts for the walnuts.

Greek Salad

Serves 4
Cost: **££** Prep time: 10 minutes **V** ✳

Ingredients
> 4 tomatoes, cut into wedges
> ½ cucumber, halved lengthways and sliced
> 1 green pepper, deseeded and cut into rings or thinly
>   sliced
> 1 onion, thinly sliced into rings
> 200g feta cheese, cubed
> 100g black stoned olives
> salt and black pepper
> 4 tablespoons (60ml) olive oil
> 1 bunch of parsley, chopped

Method
1. Arrange the salad vegetables in your serving dish/es.
2. Top with the feta and olives.
3. Season and drizzle over the oil.
4. Sprinkle with the parsley and serve.

Tip
The parsley is an integral part of this dish, not just a garnish.

Chicken and Mango Pilaff
Serves 2
Cost: ££ Prep time: 25 minutes

Ingredients
> 250g basmati rice
> 2 tablespoons (30ml) oil
> 2 leeks, sliced
> 2 medium chicken breasts, thinly sliced
> 150ml chicken stock, made with 1 stock cube and
>   boiling water
> 4 tablespoons (60ml) mango chutney
> black pepper

Method
1. Cook the rice in boiling water until tender (approximately 10 minutes).
2. Meanwhile, heat the oil and stir-fry the leeks and chicken until cooked and brown.
3. When the rice is cooked, drain well and combine with the leeks and chicken. Add the stock and chutney, mix well and cook for a few minutes until the stock is incorporated into the dish.
4. Season and serve.

Tip
This is good served with a green salad.

Quick Curry for One
Serves 1
Cost: **££** Prep time: 10 minutes + 15 minutes cooking and standing ✳

Ingredients
>1 tablespoon (15ml) oil
>1 small onion, chopped
>1/2 red pepper, deseeded and diced
>1 clove garlic, crushed
>125g minced beef
>2 teaspoons medium curry powder
>75g basmati rice
>200ml boiling water
>1 tablespoon (15ml) Indian chutney

Method
1. Heat the oil and fry the onion, pepper and garlic for 5 minutes until soft and starting to brown.
2. Add the beef and stir-fry for another 5 minutes until browned.
3. Add the rest of the ingredients and bring to the boil.
4. Cover tightly and simmer for 10 minutes.
5. Remove from the heat and leave to stand for 5 minutes before serving.

Tip
For an even more impressive curry add 1/2 teaspoon whole cumin or coriander seeds just before you add the rest of the ingredients.

Leftovers

1/2 *red pepper*
Bean Salsa (page 21)
Red Pepper and Mushroom Kebabs (page 28)
Toasted Omelette Sandwich (page 46)

Mozzarella-topped Spinach and Potato Gratin
Serves 4
Cost: ££ Prep time: 20 minutes + 55 minutes cooking **V**

Ingredients
>   600g potatoes, peeled and thinly sliced
>   500g fresh spinach, cleaned and washed
>   200g mozzarella cheese, grated
>   salt and black pepper
>   4 tomatoes, sliced
>   3 eggs, beaten
>   284ml carton whipping cream

Method
1. Preheat the oven to 180°C/350°F/Gas 4.
2. Cook the potatoes in boiling water for 5 minutes, then drain well.
3. Meanwhile, cook the spinach in boiling water for 5 minutes, drain and squeeze out excess water.
4. Grease a large casserole dish and line the bottom with half the potatoes, cover with the spinach and half the cheese, seasoning each layer well.
5. Cover with the rest of the potatoes and arrange the tomato slices on top.
6. Sprinkle with the remaining cheese.
7. Whisk together the eggs and cream, season and pour over the dish.
8. Bake in the preheated oven for 55 minutes.

Tip
It is worth getting a friend to help with the preparation of this dish. You can buy bags of grated mozzarella but this is more expensive.

Leftovers

3 eggs
Tomato and Herb Omelette (page 32)
Scrambled Curried Eggs with Chapattis (page 42)
Egg and Lentil Curry (page 50)

Italian Fish Bake
Serves 4
Cost: **£££** Prep time: 5 minutes + 30 minutes cooking

Ingredients
450g cod fillets
1 dessertspoon (10ml) lemon juice
15g butter
1 large onion, chopped
2 cloves garlic, crushed
400g can chopped tomatoes
50g stoned black olives
black pepper
100g mozzarella cheese, grated or thinly sliced

Method
1. Preheat the oven to 200°C/400°F/Gas 6.
2. Cut the fish into equal size portions and put in a greased ovenproof dish.
3. Squeeze over the lemon juice.
4. Heat the butter and fry the onion and garlic until soft and starting to brown.
5. Add the tomatoes and olives to the pan, stir well, season, then use to cover the fish.
6. Top with the cheese and bake in the preheated oven for 30 minutes until the cheese is golden.

Tip
If you have any capers add some to this dish before including the cheese.

Leftovers

Mozzarella
Chilli Pizza (page 34)
Pizza Margharita (page 34)
Aubergines Baked with Cheese (page 171)

Thai Peanutty Pork
Serves 2
Cost: £££ Prep time: 20 minutes ✳

Ingredients
>1 tablespoon (15ml) oil
>1 onion, chopped
>1 red pepper, chopped
>2 cloves garlic, crushed
>250g minced pork
>1 tablespoon (15ml) Thai red curry paste
>1 tablespoon (15ml) crunchy peanut butter
>1 tablespoon (15ml) soy sauce
>100ml water
>handful of basil, shredded (optional)
>handful of coriander (optional)

Method
1. Heat the oil and fry the onion and pepper for 5 minutes.
2. Add the garlic and pork and fry for a further 5 minutes.
3. Add the rest of the ingredients except the herbs and stir-fry for 2 minutes.
4. Stir in herbs (if using) just before serving.

Tip
This dish goes really well with noodles but can be served with rice if you prefer.

Sri Lankan Curry

Serves 4
Cost: **£££** Prep time: 30 minutes ✳

Ingredients
  1 tablespoon (15ml) oil
  1 large onion, chopped
  2 cloves garlic, crushed
  8 chicken thighs, skinned and boned, cut into cubes
  2 tablespoons (30ml) medium balti curry paste
  1 teaspoon (5ml) minced chilli
  1 teaspoon cinnamon
  200ml carton coconut cream

Method
1. Heat the oil and fry the onion and garlic until soft and browned.
2. Add the chicken and fry for another 5 minutes.
3. Add the curry paste, chilli and cinnamon and stir-fry for 1 minute.
4. Add the coconut cream, stir, cover and simmer for 5–10 minutes, until the chicken is cooked through.

Thai Prawn Curry

Serves 4
Cost: **£££** Prep time: 20 minutes ✳

Ingredients
> 1 tablespoon (15ml) oil
> 1 onion, chopped
> 1 clove garlic, crushed
> 1 teaspoon (5ml) minced ginger
> 1 tablespoon (15ml) Thai red curry paste
> 400g can coconut milk
> 450g frozen large, uncooked prawns, defrosted
> fresh coriander leaves, shredded

Method
1. Heat the oil and fry the onion, garlic and ginger until the onion is softened and starting to brown.
2. Blend in the curry paste with a little of the coconut milk, then add the rest of the coconut milk. Cook, uncovered, until the sauce has reduced and thickened a little.
3. Add the prawns and cook for a few minutes until they have cooked through (they change colour).
4. Stir in the coriander leaves and serve immediately.

Chip-topped Shepherd's Pie
Serves 2–3
Cost: **£££** Prep time: 20 minutes + 50 minutes cooking

Ingredients
> 1 tablespoon (15ml) oil
> 1 onion, chopped
> 1 carrot, diced
> 500g minced beef
> 2 teaspoons (10ml) Worcestershire sauce (optional)
> 375ml gravy, made with 60g gravy granules and
>   boiling water
> salt and black pepper
> 500g potatoes, peeled and cut into small thin chips

Method
1. Preheat the oven to 180°C/350°F/Gas 4.
2. Heat the oil and fry the onion and carrot for about 10 minutes until soft and starting to brown.
3. Add the beef and stir-fry until browned.
4. Combine the Worcestershire sauce (if using) and gravy and stir into the mince. Season.
5. Transfer to an ovenproof dish and cover with the chipped potatoes.
6. Cover tightly and cook in the preheated oven for 30 minutes.
7. Uncover, increase the temperature to 200°C/400°F/Gas 6 and cook for another 20 minutes to brown the chips.

Teriyaki Chicken Stir-fry

Serves 4

Cost: **£££** Prep and cooking time: 10 minutes + 20 minutes marinating

Ingredients

- 2 medium boneless, skinless chicken breasts, cut into thin strips
- 2 tablespoons (30ml) soy sauce
- 1 tablespoon (15ml) oil
- 2 large carrots, peeled and cut into small matchsticks
- 1 red pepper, deseeded and cut into small matchsticks
- 1 green pepper, deseeded and cut into small matchsticks
- 150g jar Sharwood's Teriyaki stir-fry sauce
- 1 bunch of spring onions, chopped

Method

1. Marinate the chicken in the soy sauce for 20 minutes.
2. Heat the oil in a frying pan and fry the chicken and marinade for 2 minutes.
3. Add the carrots and both peppers and stir-fry for 4 minutes.
4. Add the sauce and spring onions and warm through. Serve.

4 Cooking for a Crowd

Occasionally it is nice to get together with a group of friends for a really good meal and a few drinks. This might be for a specific reason or just because the sun is shining and it feels like a good idea.

Over many years I have come to the conclusion that the easiest way of entertaining large numbers is to have most of the dishes already prepared, so I rely increasingly on salads that can be made up and will sit happily for a time while other last-minute preparations are in hand. For these salads I have drawn on inspiration from many different cultures. I used to theme meals, but nowadays just mix and match as I feel like it. Luckily this coincides with the growth of 'Pacific rim' style cookery, in which West meets East, taking the best from each culture and mixing and matching to provide new and interesting menus.

These recipes cater for 8 or more.

When catering for vegetarians you can produce a feast by serving a selection of the different salads. I would serve 2 vegetarian salads as a substitute for a main course containing meat. Don't forget that even when feeding meat-eaters the main dish can also be a salad. Those containing tuna fish are great substitutes for a hot main dish.

Some points to bear in mind:

Catering for up to 8
Serve 1 starter, 2 salads and 1 main dish.

Catering for 9–12
Serve 2 starters, 3 salads and the Jambalaya (page 127).

Catering for 13–16
Serve 2 starters, 4 salads and 2 main courses.

Serve some French sticks or garlic bread alongside these dishes. As a treat you could provide a pudding. There are many to choose from in the shops, or you could make the very simple Eton Mess which is a mixture of whipped cream, strawberries and broken meringues. You will find the recipe on page 201.

I haven't given precise costings for these but at the time of writing menus made from these recipes would cost £2–2.40 per head, including a few French sticks. Some people like to get together and decide on a sum which will cover drink as well, or just share the cost of the cooking and get everyone to bring their own favourite drink (which works well if you have a mixture of heavy drinkers and teetotallers).

Some example menus would be:

Least expensive menu for 12 @ £2 per head
Chilli Olives (page 106)
Tapenade-topped Croûtes (page 107)
Potatoes in Red Pesto (page 113)
Yogurt-dressed Mushroom Salad (page 111)

Algerian Tomato and Pepper Salad (page 112)
Jambalaya (page 127)
6 French sticks

Most expensive menu for 8 @ £2.40 per head
Bruschetta (page 110)
Mushrooms à la Grecque (page 121)
Roasted Pepper Salad (page 122)
Mediterranean Lemon Chicken with Olives (page 129)
4 French sticks

Vegetarian meal for 12 @ £2.20 per head
Chilli Olives (page 106)
Caponata (page 109) and tortilla chips
Potatoes in Red Pesto (page 113)
Garlic Mushroom Salad (page 115)
Carrot, Egg and Olive Salad (page 116)
Couscous with Fruit and Nuts (page 119)
Roasted Pepper Salad (page 122)
5 French sticks

Starters

Chilli Olives
Serves 8
Prep time: 5 minutes **V Ve** ✳

Ingredients
> 200g jar green olives with lemon and mint, drained
> 2 teaspoons (10ml) minced chilli

Method
Mix together the ingredients and put in a serving bowl.

Tapenade-topped Croûtes
Makes 20–30
Prep time: 25 minutes **V Ve** ✳

Ingredients
>   7 tablespoons (100ml) olive oil
>   4 cloves garlic, crushed
>   1 French stick, sliced
>   90g jar sun-dried tomato tapenade

Method
1. Preheat the oven to 180°C/350°F/Gas 4.
2. Mix together the oil and garlic and coat each bread slice with this.
3. Lay the bread on baking sheets and bake in the pre-heated oven for 15–20 minutes until brown and crisp.
4. Serve each croûte with a little tapenade spread on top.

Tip
Watch these carefully when you bake them as they burn very easily.

Cacik *(Turkish yogurt and cucumber salad)*
Serves 8
Prep time: 10 minutes **V** ✳

Ingredients
  400g Greek yogurt
  1 cucumber, peeled and diced
  4 cloves garlic, crushed
  1 tablespoon (15ml) white wine vinegar
  salt and black pepper

Method
Mix together all the ingredients and serve.

Tip
The Greek version of this Turkish dish is Tzatziki, which is exactly the same but with 1 tablespoon fresh chopped mint added.

Caponata
Serves 8
Prep time: 10 minutes + 20 minutes cooking +
cooling **V Ve** ✳

Ingredients
> 2 aubergines, diced
> 1 onion, chopped
> 4 tablespoons (60ml) oil
> 4 large beef tomatoes, chopped
> 2 celery sticks, chopped
> 75g stoned green olives, chopped
> 2 tablespoons capers, drained and rinsed
> 4 tablespoons (60ml) white wine vinegar
> 1 tablespoon sugar

Method
1. Preheat the oven to 200°C/400°F/Gas 6.
2. Mix together the aubergines, onion and oil and spread out on a baking tray.
3. Cook in the preheated oven for 10 minutes, then add the tomatoes and cook for a further 10 minutes.
4. Remove from the oven and put into a serving dish with the rest of the ingredients (use the juices as well). Stir well and leave to cool before serving.

Leftovers

Celery
Jambalaya (page 127)
Use chopped celery in salads or mixed with cheese as a sandwich filling.

Capers
Spaghetti Putanesca (page 60)
Capers go well with any tomato-based sauces.

Bruschetta
Serves 8
Prep time: 10 minutes + 10 minutes cooking **V**

Ingredients
   1 ciabatta loaf, cut into 16 slices, toasted
   2 tablespoons (30ml) olive oil
   4 tomatoes, sliced
   200g mozzarella cheese, drained and thinly sliced
   1 teaspoon oregano
   black pepper
   100g stoned black olives

Method
1. Preheat the oven to 220°C/425°F/Gas 7.
2. Place the slices of toast in one layer on a baking tray.
3. Drizzle with 1 tablespoon (15ml) of the oil.
4. Cover with the tomatoes, then the mozzarella, sprinkle with the oregano and season.
5. Bake in the preheated oven for 10 minutes until the cheese has melted.
6. Dribble the remaining oil over the toast and garnish with the olives before serving hot.

Tip
You will need bread to mop up the juices as this is a very messy starter, but absolutely delicious!

Salads

Yogurt-dressed Mushroom Salad
Serves 8
Prep time: 5 minutes + 1 hour marinating **V** ❄

Ingredients
> 500g chestnut mushrooms, sliced
> 150g carton natural yogurt
> juice of ½ lemon
> salt and black pepper

Method
1. Mix together the mushrooms, yogurt and lemon juice. Do not season yet.
2. Leave to marinate for 1 hour.
3. Season just before serving.

Algerian Tomato and Pepper Salad
Serves 8
Prep time: 20 minutes + cooling **V Ve ✳**

Ingredients
>   3 tablespoons (45ml) olive oil
>   4 peppers of mixed colours, deseeded and sliced
>   8 tomatoes, cut into wedges
>   4 cloves garlic, crushed
>   2 teaspoons (10ml) minced chilli

Method
1. Heat the oil and fry the peppers until soft and starting to brown.
2. Add the rest of the ingredients and stir-fry until the tomatoes are just beginning to soften.
3. Place in a serving dish and leave to cool.

Potatoes in Red Pesto

Serves 8
Prep time: 15 minutes + cooling **V** ✳

Ingredients
> 1kg baby new potatoes, cooked and cooled
> 170g jar or carton fresh red pesto

Method
Mix together the potatoes and pesto and serve.

Imam Bayildi *(the priest fainted)*
Serves 8
Prep time: 20 minutes + 45 minutes cooking +
cooling **V Ve**

Ingredients
- olive oil, for frying
- 2 onions, chopped
- 4 cloves garlic, crushed
- 2 aubergines, cut into slices lengthways
- 2 × 400g cans chopped tomatoes
- 3 tablespoons (45ml) tomato purée
- 4 tablespoons fresh chopped parsley

Method
1. Preheat the oven to 180°C/350°F/Gas 4.
2. Heat 2 tablespoons (30ml) of oil and fry the onions and garlic until soft and starting to brown. Place in an ovenproof dish.
3. Heat some more oil and fry the aubergines a few slices at a time (you will need a lot of oil for this). Transfer the fried aubergines to the dish as each slice is cooked.
4. Add the remaining ingredients to the dish and bake in the preheated oven for 45 minutes.
5. Leave to cool and drizzle with a little more oil just before serving.

The story behind this Turkish dish is that the *imam* (priest) fainted when he tasted it. The miserly man was horrified at the amount of expensive olive oil his wife had used!

Garlic Mushroom Salad
Serves 8
Prep time: 5 minutes **V** ✳

Ingredients
    4 tablespoons (60ml) olive oil
    500g button mushrooms
    6 cloves garlic, crushed
    142ml carton sour cream with chives and onions
    salt and black pepper

Method
1. Heat the oil and fry the mushrooms and garlic for a few minutes – just enough to soften them.
2. Leave to cool, then combine with the sour cream. Season and serve.

Carrot, Egg and Olive Salad
Serves 8
Prep time: 20 minutes **V**

Ingredients
> 4 eggs
> 800g carrots, grated
> juice of ½ lemon
> 2 tablespoons black mustard seeds
> 3 tablespoons (45ml) oil
> 200g mixed olives, drained
> salt and black pepper

Method
1. Put the eggs in a saucepan, cover with cold water and bring to the boil.
2. Simmer for 10 minutes. Plunge into cold water to cool.
3. Peel off the shells and cut each in half lengthways.
4. Meanwhile, mix together the carrots, lemon juice and mustard seeds.
5. Heat the oil in a frying pan, add the carrot mixture and stir-fry until the carrot is just softening and the seeds begin to pop, then remove immediately.
6. Put the contents of the pan in the middle of a serving dish and surround with the egg halves and olives.
7. Season and serve.

Tip
Half the prep time of this dish is taken up by grating the carrots, so if you can get some help here you can save time.

Use the black mustard seeds to give a tang to other salads or use up when cooking curries.

Leftovers

Eggs
Kidney Bean Kedgeree (page 30)
Pipérade (page 47)
Huevos Rancheros (page 157)
Omelette (page 161)

Tabbouleh
Serves 12
Prep time: 20 minutes + 20 minutes marinating **V Ve** ✳

Ingredients
350g bulgar wheat
juice from 2 large or 4 small lemons
salt and pepper
8 tablespoons (120ml) olive oil
1 bunch of parsley, finely chopped
1 bunch of mint, finely chopped
1 bunch of spring onions, sliced
6 tomatoes, skinned and diced
½ cucumber, diced

Method
1. Soak the bulgar wheat in boiling water for 10 minutes, then drain and squeeze out as much excess water as you can. The more water you can remove, the better the finished dish will be.
2. Add the lemon juice, season well and leave to stand for 20 minutes.
3. Add the rest of the ingredients, stir and serve.

Tomato and Mozzarella Salad
Serves 8
Prep time: 10 minutes **V**

Ingredients
   8 tomatoes, sliced
   400g mozzarella cheese, sliced
   4 tablespoons (60ml) olive oil
   2 tablespoons (30ml) white wine vinegar
   pinch of sugar
   salt and black pepper

Method
1. Arrange alternate slices of tomato and cheese on each plate.
2. Put the rest of the ingredients in a screw-top jar and shake well. Drizzle the dressing all over the salad.

Tip
This is a dish where the better the oil used, the better the finished dish.

If you are serving with other dishes which use basil, keep a few sprigs back to garnish this salad.

Couscous with Fruit and Nuts
Serves 8
Prep time: 5 minutes + 20 minutes standing **V Ve** ✳

Ingredients
>   250g couscous
>   425ml vegetable stock, made with 1 stock cube and
>   boiling water
>   100g raisins
>   100g ready-to-eat apricots, chopped
>   50g toasted flaked almonds
>   juice of 1 lemon
>   juice of 1 lime
>   3 tablespoons chopped coriander
>   salt and black pepper

Method
1. Place the couscous in a bowl and pour on the hot stock.
    Leave to stand for 20 minutes until the stock is absorbed.
2. Mix in the rest of the ingredients, season and serve.

Italian Tuna and Bean Salad
Serves 8
Prep time: 10 minutes ✳

Ingredients
   4 tablespoons (60ml) olive oil
   2 onions, sliced into rings
   1 tablespoon (15ml) white wine vinegar
   1 clove garlic, crushed
   3 × 400g cans cannellini beans, drained
   2 × 185g cans tuna, drained and flaked
   salt and black pepper

Method
1. Heat 1 tablespoon (15ml) of the oil and fry the onions until soft and starting to brown.
2. Put the rest of the oil and the vinegar and garlic in a screw-top jar and shake well.
3. Gently mix together the onions, beans and tuna.
4. Drizzle with the dressing, season well and serve.

Mushrooms à la Grecque
Serves 8
Prep time: 15 minutes **V Ve** ✳

Ingredients
> 8 tablespoons (120ml) olive oil
> 2 large onions, sliced
> 2 cloves garlic, crushed
> 600g economy mushrooms
> 8 tomatoes, cut into wedges
> 100g stoned black olives
> 2 tablespoons (30ml) white wine vinegar
> salt and black pepper

Method
1. Heat 2 tablespoons (30ml) of the oil and fry the onions and garlic until soft and starting to brown.
2. Add the mushrooms and tomatoes and gently stir-fry until just softening.
3. Place in a serving dish and garnish with the olives.
4. Mix the rest of the oil with the vinegar, season and drizzle over the salad.

Roasted Pepper Salad

Serves 8
Prep time: 10 minutes + 35 minutes cooking +
cooling **V Ve** ✳

Ingredients

8 peppers of mixed colours, deseeded and sliced
2 cloves garlic, crushed
6 tablespoons (90ml) olive oil
salt and black pepper

Method

1. Preheat the oven to 220°C/425°F/Gas 7.
2. Mix together all the ingredients and season.
3. Roast in the preheated oven for 35 minutes.
4. Transfer with all the juices from the tray to a serving dish and leave to cool.

Main dishes

Stuffed Peppers
Serves 8
Prep time: 15 minutes + 65 minutes cooking **V Ve**

Ingredients
2 tablespoons (30ml) oil
1 large onion, finely chopped
2 cloves garlic, crushed
100g mushrooms, finely chopped
225g bulgar wheat
1 teaspoon cinnamon
3 heaped tablespoons raisins
400ml vegetable stock, made with 1 stock cube and
    boiling water
salt and pepper
4 red peppers, deseeded and halved lengthways

Method
1. Heat 1 tablespoon (15ml) of the oil and fry the onion and garlic for a few minutes until starting to brown.
2. Add the mushrooms and stir-fry for 2 minutes, then add all the other ingredients except the peppers and the remaining oil, stir well and bring to the boil.
3. Cover tightly and simmer for 30 minutes until the stock has been absorbed.
4. Preheat the oven to 180°C/350°F/Gas 4.
5. Place the halved peppers in a shallow ovenproof dish and use the cooked bulgar wheat mixture to stuff them.
6. Drizzle the remaining oil over the stuffed peppers.
7. Cover tightly and bake in the preheated oven for 35 minutes.

Sticky Fingers Chicken
Serves 8
Prep time: 5 minutes + 35 minutes cooking

Ingredients
 8 tablespoons (120ml) tomato ketchup
 4 tablespoons (60ml) Worcestershire sauce
 4 tablespoons (60ml) light soy sauce
 2 tablespoons (30ml) runny honey
 8 chicken drumsticks
 8 chicken thighs

Method
1. Preheat the oven to 200°C/400°F/Gas 6.
2. Mix together the tomato ketchup, Worcestershire sauce, soy sauce and honey, then use to coat the chicken pieces.
3. Lay the coated chicken in a single layer on a baking tin.
4. Bake in the preheated oven for 35 minutes until cooked and starting to blacken at the edges.

Chicken and Chickpea Stew
Serves 8
Prep time: 20 minutes + 1 hour cooking

Ingredients
3 tablespoons (45ml) oil
8 chicken thighs
8 chicken drumsticks
2 large onions, chopped
4 cloves garlic, crushed
500g jar passata (sieved tomatoes)
2 teaspoons dried thyme
400g can chickpeas, drained
salt and black pepper

Method
1. Preheat the oven to 190°C/375°F/Gas 5.
2. Heat half the oil and quickly fry 8 chicken pieces at a time. As each batch is browned, place in an ovenproof dish.
3. Fry the onions in the rest of the oil until starting to brown, then add to the dish.
4. Add the rest of the ingredients and season.
5. Cover and cook in the preheated oven for 1 hour.

Niçoise Salad
Serves 8
Prep time: 15 minutes ✳

Ingredients

For the salad
    4 eggs
    12 tomatoes, cut into wedges
    2 green peppers, deseeded and cut into thin rings
    1 cucumber, peeled and thinly sliced
    300g can broad beans, drained
    2 × 185g cans tuna, drained and flaked
    2 × 50g cans anchovy fillets, drained
    200g black olives

For the dressing
    8 tablespoons (120ml) olive oil
    3 tablespoons (45ml) white wine vinegar
    2 cloves garlic, crushed
    salt and pepper

Method
1. Place the eggs in a saucepan, cover with cold water and bring to the boil.
2. Cook for 10 minutes. Plunge into cold water to cool.
3. Peel off the shells and cut each in half lengthways.
4. Arrange all the salad ingredients in a serving dish.
5. Put the oil, vinegar and garlic in a screw-top jar and season. Shake well, then pour over the salad.

Leftovers

Eggs
Kidney Bean Kedgeree (page 30)
Toasted Omelette Sandwich (page 46)
Pipérade (page 47)
Huevos Rancheros (page 157)
Omelette (page 161)

Jambalaya
Serves 12
Prep time: 25 minutes + 15 minutes cooking

Ingredients
>   4 tablespoons (60ml) oil
>   4 medium chicken breasts, boned and skinned, cut
>   into cubes
>   150g chorizo sausage, skinned and sliced
>   1 tablespoon paprika
>   2 large onions, chopped
>   4 celery sticks, sliced
>   3 peppers of mixed colours, deseeded and cubed
>   4 cloves garlic, crushed
>   2 teaspoons (10ml) minced chilli
>   700g long-grain rice
>   4 tomatoes, cut into wedges
>   2 litres chicken stock, made with 2 stock cubes and
>   boiling water

Method
1. Heat the oil and fry the chicken, sausage and paprika for a few minutes until starting to brown.
2. Remove the meat to a large saucepan.
3. Fry the onions, celery, peppers, garlic and chilli until soft and starting to brown.
4. Add to the saucepan and start to heat through.
5. When hot, add the rice and stir through.
6. Add the tomatoes and stock. Bring to the boil, then simmer for 15 minutes until the stock is absorbed.

Tip
Although I had a pan large enough to cook this, you may need to divide it between 2 large pans.

Leftovers

Celery
Caponata (page 109)
Use celery in salads or chop and mix with cheese and use as a sandwich filling.

Chilli-dressed Tuna and Roasted Pepper Salad
Serves 8
Prep time: 15 minutes + 35 minutes cooking + cooling ✳

Ingredients

For the salad
    4 eggs
    Roasted Pepper Salad (page 122)
    2 × 185g cans tuna, drained and flaked
    200g black olives
    2 tablespoons capers

For the dressing
    4 tablespoons (60ml) olive oil
    1 tablespoon (15ml) white wine vinegar
    2 teaspoons (10ml) minced chilli
    2 cloves garlic, crushed
    salt and pepper

Method
1. Place the eggs in a saucepan, cover with cold water and bring to the boil.
2. Cook for 10 minutes. Plunge into cold water to cool.
3. Peel off the shells and cut each in half lengthways.
4. Pile all the salad ingredients into a serving dish.
5. Put the dressing ingredients into a screw-top jar and shake well, then drizzle all over the salad.

Leftovers

2 eggs
Kidney Bean Kedgeree (page 30)
Toasted Omelette Sandwich (page 46)
Pipérade (page 47)
Huevos Rancheros (page 157)
Omelette (page 161)

Mediterranean Lemon Chicken with Olives
Serves 8
Prep time: 20 minutes + 1 hour cooking ✳

Ingredients
    4 tablespoons (60ml) oil
    8 chicken legs
    2 large onions, chopped
    1 litre curried gravy, made with 150g chip shop curry
      gravy granules
    4 tablespoons (60ml) runny honey
    4 lemons, cut into wedges
    100g stoned black olives
    black pepper

Method
1. Preheat the oven to 190°C/375°F/Gas 5.
2. In a large heatproof and ovenproof pan, heat the oil and
    fry the chicken and onions until starting to brown.
3. Add the gravy and honey and bring to the boil.
4. Add the lemons, then cover and bake in the preheated
    oven for 1 hour.
5. Stir through the olives and season before serving.

5 Something Special

There are certain times when a *diner à deux* is called for or you want to whip up a special meal for someone's birthday. I have included some out-of-the-ordinary recipes here. They are a little more expensive but still shouldn't work out at more than £2–2.50 per head.

For a really simple yet stylish birthday spread for six you could use the recipe for Sabzi Curry (page 133), choose another curry sauce from this range and make a chicken curry, serve them with a salad of sliced onions and tomatoes, rice, some poppadoms and two Indian pickles and you would have a great feast.

There are also some dishes for friends who want to cook a Sunday lunch together. Here are some alternatives to Sunday roasts (which can be expensive). It's easy to produce a baked dish that can be served with some simple veg or salad. Alternatively, there's a curried chicken salad for summer days. None of the dishes for Sunday lunches should cost more than £2 per head.

Special Treats

Canoodle Noodles
Serves 2
Prep time: 15 minutes **V**

Ingredients
    125g medium egg noodles
    1 tablespoon (15ml) oil
    1 red pepper, deseeded and sliced
    200g broccoli, broken into small florets
    100g chestnut mushrooms, sliced
    50g cashew nuts
    1 teaspoon (5ml) minced ginger
    1 tablespoon (15ml) soy sauce
    1 tablespoon (15ml) runny honey

Method
1. Cook the noodles in boiling water for 4 minutes, then drain.
2. Meanwhile, preheat the grill and line the grill tray with foil.
3. Heat the oil and stir-fry the pepper, broccoli and mushrooms for 3 minutes.
4. Grill the cashews until starting to brown – but don't burn them!
5. Add the ginger, soy sauce and honey to the stir-fry and stir through.
6. Mix together all the ingredients and serve.

Sabzi Curry
Serves 2–3
Prep time: 20 minutes **V** ✳

Ingredients
- 1 tablespoon (15ml) oil
- 1 onion, thinly sliced
- 225g okra, washed and stalk ends cut off
- 100g mushrooms, sliced
- 350g jar Madhur Jaffrey's sabzi sauce
- 250g spinach, large stalks removed and roughly chopped

Method
1. Heat the oil and fry the onion for 2–3 minutes.
2. If the okra are quite long, cut the stems in two about halfway down.
3. Add the okra to the onion and fry for another 4–5 minutes.
4. Add the mushrooms and stir-fry for another minute.
5. Add the sabzi sauce and bring to the boil, stirring well.
6. Reduce the heat, cover and simmer for 3 minutes.
7. Add the spinach and keep stirring until it has wilted into the curry, then serve.

Tip
For a special occasion, this is wonderful served with rice, naan breads and Indian salads accompanied by wedges of lemons and limes and a couple of Indian pickles such as brinjal and tomato.

Coconut Chicken Curry
Serves 2
Prep time: 35 minutes ✳

Ingredients
1 tablespoon (15ml) oil
1 onion, diced
½ green pepper, deseeded and diced
350g chicken thighs, skinned
100g mushrooms, quartered
2 tablespoons (30ml) medium balti curry paste
1 teaspoon (5ml) minced lemongrass
1 teaspoon (5ml) minced ginger
2 cloves garlic, crushed
1 tablespoon (15ml) soy sauce
200ml carton coconut cream
handful of basil leaves (optional)

Method
1. Heat the oil and fry the onion and pepper for 5–10 minutes until starting to brown.
2. Add the chicken thighs and fry for another 5 minutes.
3. Add the mushrooms, curry paste, lemongrass, ginger, garlic and soy sauce and stir-fry for 2–3 minutes.
4. Add the coconut cream, stir well, cover and simmer for 5 minutes.
5. Stir in the basil (if using) just before serving.

Tip
Serve with rice and a side salad of tomatoes and onion or spinach salad.

Leftovers

½ green pepper
Chicken and Banana Creole (page 53)
Green Curry (page 88)

West Country Chicken
Serves 2
Prep time: 10 minutes + 50 minutes cooking ✳

Ingredients
    25g butter, softened
    2 tablespoons (30ml) whole-grain mustard
    1 teaspoon (5ml) Worcestershire sauce (optional)
    2 medium chicken breasts
    1 apple, cored, peeled and sliced
    ¼ Savoy cabbage, sliced
    250ml bottle dry cider

Method
1. Preheat the oven to 190°C/375°F/Gas 5.
2. Combine the butter, mustard and Worcestershire sauce (if using) and use this to coat the chicken breasts.
3. Put the apple and cabbage in an ovenproof dish and place the chicken breasts on top.
4. Pour over the cider, cover and cook in the preheated oven for 50 minutes.

Leftovers

Savoy Cabbage
Pot-roasted Chicken (page 143)
Stir-fried Greens (page 182)
Japaneasy Noodles (page 191)

Roasted Coconut Chicken
Serves 4
Prep time: 5 minutes + 1½ hours cooking ✳

Ingredients
    2 tablespoons (30ml) medium balti curry paste
    2 tablespoons (30ml) oil
    1 teaspoon (5ml) minced ginger
    1 teaspoon (5ml) minced lemongrass or finely chopped
      fresh lemongrass
    400g can coconut milk
    1.5kg free-range chicken

Method
1. Preheat the oven to 190°C/375°F/Gas 5.
2. Mix together the curry paste, oil, ginger and lemongrass with 2 tablespoons (30ml) of the coconut milk.
3. Brush the chicken all over with the paste and place any remaining paste inside the chicken.
4. Put the chicken in a roasting tin and pour over the remaining coconut milk.
5. Roast in the preheated oven for 1½ hours, basting occasionally with the coconut milk.
6. When the chicken is cooked, leave to stand for 10 minutes before carving.
7. To check the chicken is cooked, stick a sharp knife into the thigh and make sure that the juices are running clear. Any sign of pink in the juices means that the chicken needs to be cooked a little longer.

Kebabs with Satay Sauce
Serves 4
Prep time: 15 minutes + 1 hour marinating

Ingredients

For the kebabs
    2 tablespoons (30ml) medium balti curry paste
    1 tablespoon (15ml) soy sauce
    1 teaspoon (5ml) honey or sugar
    500g lean flash-fry steak, cubed

For the satay sauce
    100g crunchy peanut butter
    200ml carton creamed coconut
    1 tablespoon (15ml) lemon juice
    ½ teaspoon (2.5ml) minced chilli

Method
1. Mix together the curry paste, soy sauce and honey or sugar.
2. Add the steak and marinate for 1 hour.
3. Preheat the grill.
4. Thread the meat on to 8 wooden skewers.
5. Grill the kebabs for 8 minutes, turning once.
6. Meanwhile, mix together the sauce ingredients and heat gently, stirring until well combined.

Moroccan Meatballs with Gravy and Vegetables
Serves 6
Prep time: 15 minutes + 30 minutes cooking

Ingredients
- 2 small onions, finely chopped
- 1 heaped tablespoon raisins
- 750g minced beef
- 1 tablespoon (15ml) tomato purée
- 1 teaspoon curry powder
- 3 tablespoons (45ml) oil
- ½ teaspoon cinnamon
- 600ml curried gravy, made with 100g chip shop curry gravy granules
- juice of ½ lemon
- 2 celery sticks, thickly sliced
- 1 large or 2 medium courgettes, sliced
- 180g frozen peas

Method
1. Mix together half the onion, the raisins, beef, tomato purée and curry powder.
2. Shape the mixture into 24 meatballs.
3. Using 1 tablespoon (15ml) of the oil, fry the meatballs in small batches, until browned.
4. Tip out the excess fat and put all the meatballs in the pan.
5. Add the cinnamon, gravy and lemon juice, cover and cook for 25–30 minutes until the meatballs are cooked.
6. Heat the remaining 2 tablespoons (30ml) of oil and fry the celery and courgettes until soft and starting to brown.
7. Add the peas and continue cooking for 5 minutes until the peas are cooked.
8. Just before serving stir the vegetables into the meatballs and gravy.

Tip
You could omit the cinnamon but it is this that gives it a Moroccan flavour.

Lime-fried Chicken
Serves 6
Prep time: 20 minutes ✳

Ingredients
>   3 tablespoons (45ml) oil
>   4 medium chicken breasts, boned and skinned, cut
>   into bite-sized pieces
>   1 onion, chopped
>   2 cloves garlic, crushed
>   grated zest and juice of 2 limes
>   15g pack coriander, chopped

Method
1. Heat the oil and fry the chicken, onion and garlic for
    about 10 minutes until starting to brown.
2. Add the lime zest and juice and coriander and stir-fry for
    1 minute, then serve.

Potato Moussaka

Serves 4–6
Prep time: 25 minutes + 55 minutes cooking

Ingredients
    1kg potatoes

For the meat sauce
    2 tablespoons (30ml) oil
    2 onions, chopped
    2 cloves garlic, crushed
    500g minced lamb
    1 teaspoon ground cinnamon
    400g can chopped tomatoes
    1 teaspoon (5ml) honey or sugar
    1 teaspoon oregano
    2 tablespoons (30ml) tomato purée
    salt and black pepper

For the cheese topping
    3 eggs, beaten
    150g natural yogurt
    200g cheese, grated

Method
1. Boil the potatoes for 10 minutes, then slice thickly.
2. Heat the oil and fry the onions and garlic until starting to brown.
3. Add the lamb and cinnamon and stir-fry until the meat is browned.
4. Add the rest of the ingredients for the meat sauce and simmer gently for 15 minutes.
5. Meanwhile, preheat the oven to 200°C/400°F/Gas 6.
6. Place a layer of potatoes in an ovenproof dish, then cover with alternate layers of meat sauce and potatoes, finishing with a meat layer.
7. Beat together the eggs, yogurt and half the cheese and spoon this over the meat layer.
8. Sprinkle with the remaining cheese and cook, uncovered, in the preheated oven for 40 minutes.

Leftovers

Eggs
Tomato and Herb Omelette (page 32)
Scrambled Curried Eggs with Chapattis (page 42)
Egg and Lentil Curry (page 50)

X-tra Nice Chicken
Serves 6
Prep time: 10 minutes + 35 minutes cooking

Ingredients
>2 tablespoons (30ml) oil
>6 medium chicken breasts, boned and skinned
>knob of butter
>6 tomatoes, chopped
>3 tablespoons (45ml) whole-grain mustard
>150ml white wine or chicken stock, made with 1 stock cube and boiling water
>2 tablespoons fresh tarragon, chopped
>salt and black pepper
>100ml crème fraîche

Method
1. Preheat the oven to 180°C/350°F/Gas 4.
2. Heat the oil and fry the chicken until browned. Place in an ovenproof dish.
3. Add the butter to the pan and fry the tomatoes for 3 minutes.
4. Stir in the mustard and wine or stock, bring to the boil and pour over the chicken.
5. Sprinkle with the tarragon, season, then cover and cook for 35 minutes.
6. Stir in the crème fraîche just before serving.

Tip
You can use chopped tarragon in a cheese and herb omelette.

Leftovers

Crème fraîche
Mushroom Stroganoff (page 23)
Tricolor Spaghetti (page 58)
Eggs Florentine (page 165)

Pot-roasted Chicken
Serves 4
Prep time: 10 minutes + 1½ hours cooking ✳

Ingredients
> ½ Savoy cabbage, sliced
> 1 large leek, sliced
> 1.7–2kg free-range chicken
> 1 chicken stock cube
> sprinkling of dried thyme
> 25g butter

Method
1. Preheat the oven to 200°C/400°F/Gas 6.
2. Put the cabbage and leek in a large casserole dish and place the chicken on top.
3. Make up the stock cube with 300ml boiling water, then add the thyme.
4. Pour the stock over the chicken and dot with pieces of butter.
5. Cover and cook in the preheated oven for 1 hour. Remove the cover and cook for another 30 minutes.
6. Divide the chicken and vegetables between 4 plates, spoon over the cooking liquid and serve.

Tip
This is best served with baking potatoes which have the bonus of being cooked alongside the chicken.

If you don't have a casserole dish use a roasting tin and cover it with roasting foil.

Leftovers

Savoy cabbage
West Country Chicken (page 135)
Stir-fried Greens (page 182)
Japaneasy Noodles (page 191)

Winter Warmer

Serves 4–6
Prep time: 20 minutes + 50 minutes cooking

Ingredients
    700g potatoes, thickly sliced
    1 tablespoon (15ml) oil
    2 onions, peeled and cut into rings
    1 tablespoon demerara sugar
    1 teaspoon (5ml) white wine vinegar
    2 × 400g cans frankfurters, drained and sliced
    400g can butter beans, drained
    2 tablespoons (30ml) whole-grain mustard
    200ml crème fraîche

Method
1. Preheat the oven to 190°C/375°F/Gas 5.
2. Cook the potatoes in boiling water for just 5 minutes, then drain well.
3. Meanwhile, heat the oil and fry the onions for a few minutes until soft and starting to brown. Add the sugar and white wine vinegar and continue to cook until a deep brown colour.
4. Mix together the onions, frankfurters, butter beans, mustard and 4 tablespoons of the crème fraîche and place in an ovenproof dish.
5. Cover with the potato slices and spoon over the rest of the crème fraîche.
6. Bake in the preheated oven for 50 minutes until the top is golden brown.

Veggie Winter Warmer
Serves 4–6
Prep time: 15 minutes + 50 minutes cooking **V**

Ingredients
> 700g potatoes, thickly sliced
> 2 tablespoons (30ml) oil
> 2 onions, chopped
> 560g veggie sausages, defrosted and cut into chunks
> 2 × 400g cans chilli beans
> 200ml vegetable stock, made with 1 stock cube and
>   boiling water
> 1 tablespoon (15ml) whole-grain mustard
> 50g butter
> salt and black pepper

Method
1. Preheat the oven to 190°C/375°F/Gas 5.
2. Boil the potatoes for 5 minutes, then drain well.
3. Heat the oil and fry the onions and sausages until starting to brown.
4. Mix together the onions, sausages, chilli beans and stock and place in a shallow ovenproof dish. Cover with the potatoes.
5. Mix together the mustard and butter and spoon over the potatoes. Season.
6. Bake, uncovered, in the preheated oven for 50 minutes.

Vegetarian Pasta Bake
Serves 6
Prep time: 35 minutes + 25 minutes cooking **V**

Ingredients
    4 tablespoons (60ml) oil
    1 onion, chopped
    3 peppers of mixed colours, deseeded and cubed
    2 courgettes, halved and sliced
    250g mushrooms, sliced
    400g can chopped tomatoes
    1 tablespoon (15ml) tomato purée
    4 sun-dried tomatoes, sliced
    1 teaspoon dried oregano
    salt and pepper
    300g penne pasta
    350ml ready-made cheese sauce
    50g Cheddar cheese, grated

Method
1. Preheat the oven to 190°C/375°F/Gas 5.
2. Heat the oil and fry the onion for about 5 minutes until starting to brown.
3. Add the peppers, courgettes and mushrooms and fry for another 10 minutes.
4. Add the tomatoes, tomato purée, sun-dried tomatoes and oregano. Season and simmer for 10 minutes.
5. Meanwhile, cook the pasta in boiling water according to the packet instructions, then drain.
6. Put the sauced vegetables in a large ovenproof dish. Mix the pasta with the cheese sauce and spoon over the vegetables.
7. Sprinkle with the cheese and bake in the preheated oven for 25 minutes until golden brown on top.

Garlic Chicken
Serves 6
Prep time: 1 hour

Ingredients
>6 chicken legs
>1 tablespoon (15ml) oil
>1 onion, diced
>3 tablespoons (45ml) white wine vinegar
>400g can chopped tomatoes
>4 cloves garlic, crushed
>1 tablespoon paprika
>½ teaspoon dried thyme
>salt and black pepper
>100ml crème fraîche

Method
1. Preheat the oven to 180°C/350°F/Gas 4.
2. Put the chicken in a large ovenproof tin or casserole dish.
3. Heat the oil and fry the onion until just starting to brown.
4. Add with the rest of the ingredients, except the crème fraîche, to the chicken.
5. Season, cover with a tightly fitting lid or foil and cook in the preheated oven for 55 minutes.
6. Stir in the crème fraîche just before serving.

Leftovers

Crème fraîche
Mushroom Stroganoff (page 23)
Tricolor Spaghetti (page 58)
Eggs Florentine (page 165)

Spinach and Red Pesto Bake
Serves 6
Prep time: 10 minutes + 35 minutes cooking **V**

Ingredients
225g baby spinach
142ml carton double cream
salt and black pepper
6 slices white bread, crusts removed and sliced
   diagonally
175g jar red pesto sauce
250g Cheddar cheese, grated
3 eggs, beaten
450ml milk

Method
1. Preheat the oven to 190°C/375°F/Gas 5.
2. Cook the spinach in boiling water for a few minutes to wilt it, then drain well and squeeze out as much water as you can. Mix with the cream and season.
3. Use 2 slices of bread to cover the bottom of an oven-proof dish.
4. Spoon in half the red pesto sauce, spread over the bread and cover with half the creamed spinach. Sprinkle with one-third of the cheese.
5. Cover with 2 more slices of bread and spread these with the remaining red pesto sauce, the remaining creamed spinach and half the remaining cheese.
6. Top with the last 2 slices of bread.
7. Mix together the eggs and milk and season. Pour over the bread, then sprinkle with the remaining cheese.
8. Bake in the preheated oven for 35 minutes.

Tip
You can vary this bake by substituting other sauces for the red pesto. We made a lovely one with an aubergine and pepper sauce.

Leftovers

Eggs
Tomato and Herb Omelette (page 32)
Scrambled Curried Eggs with Chapattis (page 42)
Egg and Lentil Curry (page 50)

Roasted Chicken and Vegetables
Serves 6
Prep time: 15 minutes + 65 minutes cooking

Ingredients
- 6 chicken drumsticks
- 6 chicken thighs
- salt and black pepper
- 3 peppers of mixed colours, deseeded and cut into strips
- 450g sweet potatoes, cut into small chips
- 2 tablespoons (30ml) oil
- 200ml chicken stock, made with 1 stock cube and boiling water
- 2 cloves garlic, crushed
- 1 tablespoon (15ml) tomato purée
- 3 tomatoes, halved
- 2 slices bread, crumbed
- 1 bunch of green parsley, finely chopped

Method
1. Preheat the oven to 190°C/375°F/Gas 5.
2. Put the chicken pieces in a large roasting tin and season.
3. Place the peppers and potatoes in a large bowl and add the oil. Mix well so all the vegetables have a coating of oil, then season and place in the roasting tin.
4. Roast the chicken and vegetables in the preheated oven for 50 minutes.
5. Mix together the hot stock, garlic and tomato purée and pour over the chicken and vegetables.
6. Place the tomatoes in the tin, mix together the breadcrumbs and parsley and sprinkle over the dish.
7. Return to the oven for 15 minutes until the topping has browned. Serve.

Tip
The parsley is an integral ingredient in this dish, not a garnish. You can buy it pre-chopped now if you wish, but this is more expensive.

Coronation Chicken Salad

Serves 6
Prep time: 10 minutes ✳

Ingredients
> 4 roasted chicken breasts, skin removed and meat cut into strips
> 300g jar coronation dressing
> 3 bananas, sliced
> 50g ready-to-eat apricots, diced
> 1 heaped tablespoon raisins
> 1 bunch of spring onions, sliced
> 1 bunch of watercress
> iceberg lettuce leaves, shredded
> salt and black pepper

Method
1. Mix together the chicken, dressing, bananas, apricots and raisins.
2. Place the spring onions, watercress and lettuce in a serving dish.
3. Spoon the coronation chicken on to the salad. Season and serve.

6 Simple Budget Standbys

These are the cheapest recipes in the book. When your money is running out these are the ones to turn to.

Here you will also find a survival guide for the last week of term when the money is gone and your overdraft has come to a close. I recommend that you buy yourself £15 worth of supermarket stamps/coupons at the start of term while you still have money, then when you're really desperate you will still be able to eat that last week. (As long as you haven't lost them!) Don't forget at the end of term to claim your customer loyalty card tokens or vouchers if you've saved them by shopping at the same supermarket regularly. By planning ahead you will still be able to have a healthy diet right to the end of term, otherwise you'll probably end up eating plain pasta, night after night (with not a piece of fruit or veg to be seen as all your money will be gone).

The dishes in this chapter that feed one, two or three can be made for 75p or less per head and those for four will work out at 50p or less per head.

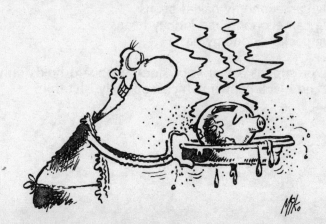

Survival Guide

Shopping list

2 × 1 litre economy cartons of orange juice
2.27 litres milk
300g Cheddar cheese
250g butter (use sparingly in sandwiches and substitute
  for oil in cooking)
½ dozen free-range eggs
125g tub soft cheese with garlic
1 large loaf bread
6 tomatoes
½ cucumber
3 onions
100g mushrooms
2 chillis
1 small leek
1 small courgette
225g broccoli
1 large baking potato
900g apples ⎫
900g bananas ⎭ 14 pieces of fruit in total
750g economy branflakes
400g can economy tomatoes
400g can economy baked beans
400g can economy red kidney beans
500g packet economy pasta

This presupposes that your stock cupboard holds only
salt and black pepper, which hopefully isn't true.

Meal Plan

Breakfast each day
Branflakes and milk, orange juice

Lunch each day
Sandwich of grated cheese and cucumber or sliced tomato
Banana or apple

Evening meals
Huevos Rancheros (page 157) and 2 slices bread
Student Standby (page 156) and pasta
Creamed Leek and Courgette Sauce (page 159) and pasta
Omelette (page 161) with cheese and tomato, 2 slices bread
Broccoli Sauce (page 159) and pasta
2 scrambled eggs, baked beans and 2 slices toast
Chilli and Garlic Beans (page 158) with a baked potato

Serve orange juice with the evening meal and follow with another apple or banana

This is a healthy eating plan which when I was writing this book came to £13.90. So it is just possible to exist on £2 per day, even on campus (as long as you can get to a superstore) and still have a healthy diet. However, this is fairly restrictive and don't forget that unless in dire financial straits you will want money for drinks such as tea, coffee or Coke around campus and therefore most students would normally need to budget to spend around £28 per week.

Student Standby
Serves 1
Cost: £ Prep time: 20 minutes **V** ✳

Ingredients
1 tablespoon (15ml) oil
1 onion, chopped
1 clove garlic, crushed (optional)
100g mushrooms, sliced
1 tomato, cut into wedges
25g cheese, grated
salt and black pepper

Method
1. Heat the oil and fry the onion, garlic and mushrooms until soft and starting to brown.
2. Add the tomato and cook for a few minutes until just softening.
3. Stir in the cheese, season and serve.

Tip
Use as a topping for pasta.

Huevos Rancheros
Serves 1
Cost: **£** Prep time: 10 minutes **V**

Ingredients
    400g can plum tomatoes, drained and flesh chopped,
       reserving half the juice
    1 teaspoon (5ml) minced chilli
    oil, for frying
    2 eggs

Method
1. Place the tomatoes, juice and chilli in a small saucepan and heat gently for 10 minutes, until reduced to a sauce.
2. Heat enough oil in a frying pan to just cover the bottom.
3. Gently break the eggs into the pan. Baste with oil until the yolks become opaque.
4. Spoon the sauce on to a plate and arrange the fried eggs on top.

Leftovers

Eggs
Chinese Omelette Rolls (page 25)
Kidney Bean Kedgeree (page 30)
Toasted Omelette Sandwich (page 46)
Pipérade (page 47)
Omelette (page 161)

Chilli and Garlic Beans
Serves 1
Cost: **£** Prep time: 15 minutes **V** ✳

Ingredients
> 1 tablespoon (15ml) oil
> 1 onion, thinly sliced
> 1 chilli, deseeded and finely chopped
> 35g soft cheese with garlic
> 400g can economy red kidney beans, drained

Method
1. Heat the oil and fry the onion until soft and starting to brown.
2. Add the rest of the ingredients and continue cooking until the cheese melts down into a sauce.

Tip
Serve over pasta or with a baked potato.

Creamed Leek and Courgette Sauce
(for pasta)
Serves 1
Cost: £ Prep time: 5 minutes **V** ✳

Ingredients
>1 tablespoon (15ml) oil
>1 small leek, thinly sliced
>1 small courgette, thinly sliced
>40g soft cheese with garlic
>black pepper

Method
1. Heat the oil and fry the leek and courgette until soft and starting to brown.
2. Add the cheese and melt down until you have a creamy sauce.
3. Season and serve on your favourite pasta.

Tip
You can also use this recipe to make a Broccoli Sauce for pasta. Just substitute an onion for the leek and 225g cooked broccoli for the courgette.

Leftovers

Soft cheese with garlic
Garlicky Beans (page 38)
Chickpeas and Veg (page 160)

Chickpeas and Veg
Serves 2
Cost: **£** Prep time: 15 minutes **V** ✳

Ingredients
    1 tablespoon (15ml) oil
    1 onion, chopped
    1 courgette, halved and sliced
    40g soft cheese with garlic
    400g can chickpeas, drained

Method
1. Heat the oil and fry the onion and courgette until soft and starting to brown.
2. Add the cheese and melt down to a sauce. Stir in the chickpeas and serve.

Tip
Use as a topping for baked potatoes or pasta.

Leftovers

Soft cheese with garlic
Garlicky Beans (page 38)

Omelette *(cheese and tomato)*
Serves 2
Cost: **£** Prep time: 5 minutes **V** ✳

Ingredients
    4 eggs, beaten
    salt and black pepper
    1 tablespoon (15ml) oil
    50g cheese, grated
    2 tomatoes, chopped

Method
1. Season the eggs.
2. Heat the oil in a frying pan, pour in the eggs and keep drawing the edges of the omelette from the sides of the pan so that uncooked egg can run underneath. The omelette should only take 2–3 minutes to set.
3. Add the cheese and tomatoes and fold in half.
4. Slide the omelette on to a dish, cut in half and serve.

Tip
You can vary the toppings using whatever you have in the fridge. Cooked mushrooms and broccoli make a good filling, or chopped ham (with or without grated cheese). To make an omelette for one person, just halve the ingredients.

Leftovers

Eggs
Kidney Bean Kedgeree (page 30)
Toasted Omelette Sandwich (page 46)
Pipérade (page 47)
Huevos Rancheros (page 157)

Tikka Masala Sauce
Serves 2
Cost: **£** Prep time: 15 minutes **V** ✳

Ingredients
    1 tablespoon (15ml) oil
    1 onion, chopped
    2 cloves garlic, crushed
    2 tablespoons (30ml) tikka seasoning
    150g carton natural yogurt
    142ml carton double cream

Method
1. Heat the oil and fry the onion and garlic until soft and starting to brown. Stir in the tikka seasoning and cook for 1 minute.
2. Add the yogurt and cream and heat gently.

Tip
Use to cover cooked chicken or a mixture of cooked vegetables or warmed canned beans.

Spaghetti Tunagnese
Serves 2
Cost: £ Prep time: 20 minutes

Ingredients
>   150g spaghetti
>   142ml carton single cream
>   25g Cheddar cheese, finely grated
>   100g can tuna, drained and flaked
>   salt
>   Worcestershire sauce to taste (optional)
>   ½ bunch of spring onions, chopped

Method
1. Cook the spaghetti in a large saucepan of boiling water according to the packet instructions, then drain.
2. Put the cream in a small milkpan and bring to the boil, then gently simmer for 5 minutes.
3. Take the cream off the heat and add the cheese, blending well to make a smooth sauce.
4. Add the rest of the ingredients and heat through gently. Serve with the spaghetti.

Tip
This is even more delicious if topped with shavings of Parmesan cheese (use a potato peeler) and some freshly ground black pepper.

Leftovers

Spring onions
Bean Salsa (page 21)
Chicken Chow Mein (page 33)
Avocado and Salsa Tortillas (page 39)
Thai Lamb (page 52)

Vegetables in Creamy Mustard Sauce with Chorizo
Serves 2
Cost: £ Prep time: 10 minutes + 20 minutes cooking ✳

Ingredients
>   2 tablespoons (30ml) oil
>   1 onion, chopped
>   225g potatoes, peeled and thinly sliced
>   2 carrots, peeled and thinly sliced
>   300ml vegetable stock, made with 1 stock cube and
>   boiling water
>   142ml carton single cream
>   1 dessertspoon (10ml) whole-grain mustard
>   50g chorizo sausage, thinly sliced
>   salt and black pepper

Method
1. Heat the oil and fry the onion and potatoes for a few minutes until softening and starting to brown.
2. Add the carrots and stock, cover tightly and cook for 20 minutes until the vegetables are cooked.
3. Just before serving, stir in the other ingredients, season, warm through and serve.

Tip
Serve with rice.

Other cooked sausages can be substituted for the chorizo.

Eggs Florentine
Serves 3
Cost: £ Prep time: 5 minutes **V** ✳

Ingredients
>   250g spinach
>   50ml crème fraîche
>   black pepper
>   1 tablespoon (15ml) oil
>   6 eggs

Method
1. Wash the spinach and place in a large saucepan with 3 tablespoons (45ml) of water.
2. Turn up the heat and cook for 2–3 minutes until the spinach has wilted down.
3. Stir in the crème fraîche, season and keep warm while you heat the oil and fry the eggs.
4. Serve the eggs on the spinach.

Tip
Serve with pasta or rice.

Leftovers

Crème fraîche
Mushroom Stroganoff (page 23)
Tricolor Spaghetti (page 58)

Vegetable and Lentil Soup
Serves 4
Cost: £ Prep time: 10 minutes + 25 minutes
cooking **V Ve** ✳

Ingredients
>   500g potatoes, peeled and diced
>   1 carrot, halved and sliced
>   1 onion, chopped
>   1.2 litres vegetable stock, made with 2 stock cubes
>   and boiling water
>   400g can lentils, drained

Method
1. Put all the ingredients in a large saucepan and bring to the boil.
2. Cover and simmer for 25 minutes.
3. Squash some of the vegetables against the side of the saucepan to thicken the soup a little.
4. Serve with crusty bread.

Mascarpone and Tomato Sauce
(for pasta)
Serves 4
Cost: **£** Prep time: 15 minutes **V** ✳

Ingredients
>1 tablespoon (15ml) oil
>1 onion, chopped
>2 cloves garlic, crushed
>500g jar passata (sieved tomatoes)
>100g mascarpone cheese
>black pepper

Method
1. Heat the oil and fry the onion and garlic until browned.
2. Add the passata and simmer for 4 minutes.
3. Stir in the mascarpone and keep stirring until it has been incorporated into the sauce.
4. Season and serve mixed into your favourite pasta.

Tip
I sometimes add some sliced sun-dried tomatoes to this when I add the passata.

Leftovers

Mascarpone
Mascarpone Macaroni Cheese (page 172)

Tomato, Leek and Bacon Rice
Serves 4
Cost: £ Prep time: 25 minutes ✳

Ingredients
    2 tablespoons (30ml) oil
    2 large leeks, sliced
    1 clove garlic, crushed
    125g bacon, chopped
    400g can chopped tomatoes
    250g long-grain rice
    700ml chicken stock, made with 1 stock cube and
       boiling water
    black pepper

Method
1. Heat the oil and fry the leeks, garlic and bacon for a few minutes until soft and starting to brown.
2. Add the tomatoes and rice and cook for 1 minute.
3. Add the stock, season and cook until the rice is cooked and the stock absorbed.
4. Stir and serve immediately.

Bean Paprikash
Serves 4
Cost: **£** Prep time: 20 minutes **V** ✳

Ingredients
    1 tablespoon (15ml) oil
    2 onions, chopped
    2 dessertspoons paprika
    200ml carton crème fraîche
    400g can economy baked beans
    400g can economy red kidney beans, drained
    salt and black pepper

Method
1. Heat the oil and fry the onions until soft and browned.
2. Add the paprika and crème fraîche.
3. Gently simmer for 5 minutes, then stir in both types of beans. Heat through, season and serve.

Lebanese Salad
Serves 4
Cost: **£** Prep time: 35 minutes **V Ve**

Ingredients
  100g Puy lentils
  1 tablespoon (15ml) tomato purée
  1½ pints (800ml) vegetable stock, made with 1 stock
    cube and boiling water
  100g bulgar wheat
  juice of 1 lemon
  salt and black pepper
  1 tablespoon (15ml) oil
  2 onions, sliced
  1 teaspoon sugar
  1 bunch of fresh mint, chopped
  3 tomatoes, cut into wedges

Method
1. Put the lentils, tomato purée and stock in a pan and bring
   to the boil.
2. Cover tightly and simmer for 20 minutes.
3. Add the bulgar wheat and lemon juice and season.
4. Cook for 10 minutes until the stock has been absorbed.
5. Meanwhile, heat the oil and fry the onions and sugar
   until deep brown and caramelised.
6. Stir the mint into the lentil and bulgar wheat mixture.
7. Serve the salad topped with the fried onions and tomato
   wedges.

Tip
You can also make this substituting coriander for the mint.

Aubergines Baked with Cheese
Serves 4
Cost: £ Prep time: 20 minutes + 40 minutes cooking **V**

Ingredients
>2 aubergines, sliced in half lengthways
>3 tablespoons (45ml) olive oil
>1 onion, chopped
>1 clove garlic, crushed
>220g can chopped tomatoes
>1 tablespoon (15ml) tomato purée
>100g mozzarella cheese, cut into 8 thin slices
>black pepper

Method
1. Preheat the oven to 200°C/400°F/Gas 6.
2. Coat the aubergines with 2 tablespoons (30ml) of the oil and place on a baking tray.
3. Roast in the preheated oven for 25 minutes.
4. Meanwhile, fry the onion and garlic in the remaining oil until soft and starting to brown.
5. Add the tomatoes and tomato purée and simmer for approximately 5–10 minutes until the sauce has thickened.
6. Remove the aubergines from the oven and cover each half with some sauce and 2 of the cheese slices.
7. Season and return to the oven for 10–15 minutes to melt the cheese.

Leftovers

Mozzarella
Chilli Pizza (page 34)
Pizza Margharita (page 34)
Italian Fish Bake (page 96)

Mascarpone Macaroni Cheese
Serves 4
Cost: £ Prep time: 10 minutes **V**

Ingredients
>   250g quick-cook macaroni
>   100g mascarpone cheese
>   100ml milk
>   2 teaspoons (10ml) Dijon mustard
>   salt and black pepper
>   100g cheese, grated

Method
1. Cook the macaroni in boiling water according to the packet instructions, then drain.
2. Meanwhile, gently heat the mascarpone, milk and mustard until melted into a sauce. Season with salt and black pepper.
3. Serve the macaroni with the cheese sauce spooned over and sprinkled with the cheese.

Leftovers

Mascarpone
Mascarpone and Tomato Sauce for pasta (page 167).

Potato and Tomato Curry

Serves 4

Cost: **£** Prep time: 30 minutes **V Ve** ✳

Ingredients

    2 tablespoons (30ml) oil
    2 onions, chopped
    2 cloves garlic, crushed
    700g potatoes, peeled and cubed
    4 tablespoons medium curry powder
    6 tomatoes, cut into wedges
    300ml vegetable stock, made with 1 stock cube and
        boiling water.

Method

1. Heat the oil and fry the onions and garlic until starting to brown.
2. Add the potatoes and curry powder, stir in, then add the tomatoes and stock.
3. Bring to the boil, cover tightly and simmer for 20–25 minutes until the potatoes are cooked.

Pasta with Roasted Veg
Serves 4
Cost: **£** Prep time: 10 minutes + 40 minutes
cooking **V Ve**

Ingredients
> 800g mixed vegetables including red pepper, onion,
> courgettes, mushrooms, tomatoes
> 1 clove garlic, crushed
> sprinkling of dried thyme
> oil
> 350g pasta – bows or spirals are very good

Method
1. Preheat the oven to its highest temperature.
2. Slice, halve or roughly dice the vegetables.
3. Put them in a bowl with the garlic and thyme and use just enough oil to coat them all.
4. Transfer to a roasting sheet and cook, uncovered, in the preheated oven for 30–40 minutes until soft and blackening at the edges.
5. Meanwhile, cook the pasta according to the packet instructions.
6. Drain the pasta and serve topped with the roasted vegetables.

Tip
Non-vegans can add some grated cheese to the finished dish.

One-pan Ratatouille
Serves 6
Cost: £ Prep time: 10 minutes + 20 minutes
cooking **V Ve** ✳

Ingredients
>   100ml oil
>   2 onions, chopped
>   1 aubergine, halved and sliced
>   2 large courgettes, halved and sliced
>   1 red pepper, deseeded and cubed
>   1 yellow pepper, deseeded and cubed
>   2 cloves garlic, crushed
>   400g can chopped tomatoes
>   salt and black pepper

Method
1. Heat the oil in a large pan until very hot and stir-fry all the vegetables except the tomatoes for a few minutes.
2. Add the tomatoes, season and stir well.
3. Cover tightly and simmer for 20 minutes until all the vegetables are cooked.

Tip
This is a lot of oil for one dish but the vegetables need this. Since you taste the oil more in the finished dish, the better oil you use, such as olive, the better the finished dish will be.

You can also use this recipe to make Ratatouille Gratin: preheat the grill, transfer the ratatouille to a shallow oven-proof dish and sprinkle with 4 tablespoons white bread-crumbs and 4 tablespoons grated cheese. Grill until the top is golden brown.

Cauliflower Cheese and Bean Gratin
Serves 4
Cost: £ Prep time: 20 minutes **V**

Ingredients
  1 small cauliflower, divided into florets
  400g can red kidney beans, drained
  400g can chickpeas, drained
  350ml ready-made cheese sauce
  salt and black pepper
  2 tablespoons breadcrumbs
  50g Cheddar cheese, grated

Method
1. Cook the cauliflower in boiling water for about 10 minutes until tender, then drain.
2. Mix with the beans, chickpeas and cheese sauce, season and place in a heatproof dish.
3. Preheat the grill.
4. Mix together the breadcrumbs and cheese and sprinkle over the dish.
5. Grill until the top is bubbling and brown.

7 Etc, Etc . . .

If you want to push the boat out a little, here are some different ways of cooking those staples such as rice, noodles and potato. There's even a recipe for mashed potato and olive oil as seen in a number of trendy restaurants now.

I haven't included many vegetable dishes as most students have to keep their meals simple to save money, but I do recommend the Baked Tomatoes in Cheesy Cream (page 185) as an accompaniment to a simple chicken or meat dish. It really is to die for.

You will also find a couple of desserts for special occasions: a fruit crumble (page 200) to serve after Sunday lunch, Eton Mess (page 201) for a very special dessert that is incredibly easy to make, and a yogurt concoction (page 199) to help use up any bits and pieces in your food store. There is also my simplest version yet of the humble flapjack (page 203) and a easy recipe for rock buns (page 202). Nothing here will come to more than 50p per portion.

Cucumber Raita
Serves 2–3
Prep time: 5 minutes **V** ✳

Ingredients
    ½ cucumber, skinned and chopped
    150g carton natural yogurt

Method
Stir the cucumber into the yogurt. You can chill or serve immediately.

Tip
Serve with any spicy food (especially Indian or Mexican) as a cooling side dish.

You can make a Mint Raita by omitting the cucumber and adding a little tikka powder and chopped mint.

Peanut Butter Sauce
Serves 4
Prep time: 5 minutes **V** ✳

Ingredients
> 6 tablespoons peanut butter
> 6 tablespoons (90ml) water
> 1 tablespoon (15ml) soy sauce
> 2 teaspoons (10ml) runny honey
> black pepper

Method
In a small saucepan, gently heat all the ingredients until you have a smooth sauce.

Tip
You can make this with smooth or crunchy peanut butter.

French Dressing
Serves 4
Prep time: 5 minutes **V Ve** ✳

Ingredients
    4 tablespoons (60ml) oil
    1 tablespoon (15ml) white wine vinegar
    1 teaspoon (5ml) Dijon mustard
    pinch of caster sugar
    salt and black pepper

Method
Put all the ingredients in a screw-top jar and shake well.

Mustard-dressed Mixed Salad
Serves 4
Prep time: 5 minutes **V Ve** ✳

Ingredients

For the salad
    1 round lettuce
    100g mushrooms, sliced
    125g packet radishes, sliced
    1 carrot, grated
    1 heaped tablespoon raisins
    1 heaped tablespoon sunflower seeds

For the dressing
    6 tablespoons (90ml) olive oil
    2 tablespoons (30ml) white wine vinegar
    1 clove garlic, crushed
    2 teaspoons (10ml) whole-grain mustard
    1 teaspoon (15ml) Dijon mustard
    salt and black pepper

Method
1. Combine all the salad ingredients in a large salad bowl.
2. Put all the dressing ingredients in a screw-top jar and shake well, then use to dress the salad.

Stir-fried Greens
Serves 4
Prep time: 10 minutes **V Ve** ✳

Ingredients
>	2 tablespoons (30ml) oil
>	½ Savoy cabbage, shredded
>	250g spinach, shredded if large leaved
>	2 cloves garlic, crushed
>	2 teaspoons (10ml) minced ginger
>	2 tablespoons (30ml) soy sauce

Method
1.	Heat the oil and stir-fry the cabbage, spinach and garlic until the spinach is just starting to wilt.
2.	Add the ginger and soy sauce, stir through and serve.

Tip
This recipe is easily adapted to serve 2 people: just halve the ingredients.

Leftovers

Savoy cabbage
West Country Chicken (page 135)
Pot-roasted Chicken (page 143)
Japaneasy Noodles (page 191)

Stir-fried Courgettes
Serves 6
Prep time: 15 minutes **V Ve**. ✳

Ingredients
> 3 tablespoons (45ml) oil
> 2 large or 4 medium courgettes, sliced
> 3 garlic cloves, crushed
> 1 bunch of spring onions, sliced
> salt and black pepper

Method
1. Heat the oil and fry the courgettes and garlic for 8 minutes until starting to brown.
2. Add the spring onions and stir-fry for another 2 minutes.
3. Season and serve.

Stir-fried Celery and Walnuts
Serves 6
Prep time: 10 minutes **V** ✳

Ingredients
    knob of butter
    1 bunch of celery, trimmed and chopped diagonally
    75g walnut pieces
    2 tablespoons demerara sugar

Method
1. Melt the butter and stir-fry the celery for 2 minutes.
2. Add the walnuts and sugar and stir until the sugar caramelises.

Tip
This is excellent as an accompaniment to any roasted or grilled meats or poultry.

Baked Tomatoes in Cheesy Cream
Serves 6
Prep time: 5 minutes + 35 minutes cooking **V** ✳

Ingredients
> 500g small tomatoes, halved
> 100g Gruyère cheese, grated
> 284ml carton whipping cream
> black pepper

Method
1. Preheat the oven to 190°C/375°F/Gas 5.
2. Arrange the tomatoes in a shallow ovenproof dish, cut side uppermost.
3. Sprinkle with the cheese and pour over the cream.
4. Season and bake in the preheated oven for 35 minutes until starting to brown.
5. These are best served warm.

Tip
Tuck some fresh herbs in with the tomatoes, if you have some.

You can use this as a main course for 2–3 people if you serve it with some bread or rice.

Wedgy Potatoes
Serves 2
Prep time: 5 minutes + 45 minutes cooking **V Ve** ✳

Ingredients
    2 large potatoes
    2 tablespoons (30ml) oil
    ½ teaspoon paprika
    1 clove garlic, crushed
    salt and pepper

Method
1. Preheat the oven to 200°C/400°F/Gas 6.
2. Cut each potato into 8 wedges.
3. Put all the ingredients into a bowl and stir thoroughly to ensure the potato wedges are covered with oil.
4. Tip on to a roasting tray and cook in the preheated oven for 45 minutes until browned and cooked through.

Tip
These make a change from jacket potatoes and also make a tasty snack when served with a dip and some salad.

Roasted New Potatoes
Serves 4
Prep time: 10 minutes + 30 minutes cooking **V Ve** ✳

Ingredients
    450g new potatoes, unpeeled
    2 tablespoons (30ml) oil
    1 clove garlic, crushed
    1 tablespoon chopped fresh parsley (optional)
    salt and black pepper

Method
1. Preheat the oven to 180°C/350°F/Gas 4.
2. Cook the potatoes in boiling water for 5 minutes, then drain well.
3. Mix together all the ingredients in a bowl, so that all are well covered in oil.
4. Tip the contents of the bowl on to a baking tray and roast for 30 minutes until the potatoes are well browned.

Tip
Other herbs such as basil or rosemary could be substituted for the parsley.

Mashed Potato with Garlic and Olive Oil
Serves 6
Prep time: 30 minutes **V Ve** ✳

Ingredients
> 700g potatoes, peeled and cut into chunks
> 10 tablespoons (150ml) olive oil
> juice of ½ lemon
> 2 cloves garlic, crushed
> salt and black pepper

Method
1. Cook the potatoes in boiling water until tender (about 15–20 minutes), then drain well.
2. Mash with a potato masher or fork.
3. Gradually add the other ingredients and work them in.
4. Season and serve.

Tomato and Sweet Potato Gratin
Serves 6
Prep time: 5 minutes + 1 hour 20 minutes cooking **V** ✳

Ingredients
1 tablespoon (15ml) oil
500g tomatoes, sliced
500g sweet potatoes, sliced
pinch of dried oregano
50g Gruyère cheese, grated
salt and pepper

Method
1. Preheat the oven to 190°C/375°F/Gas 5.
2. Place the oil, tomatoes and potatoes in a large ovenproof dish.
3. Cover tightly and bake in the preheated oven for 1 hour.
4. Remove the cover, sprinkle with the oregano and cheese, season and bake, uncovered, for another 20 minutes until brown on top.

Swedish Anchovy Potato Pie
Serves 6
Prep time: 25 minutes + 1 hour cooking

Ingredients
　　2 tablespoons (30ml) oil
　　2 onions, sliced
　　50g can anchovy fillets, drained
　　284ml carton whipping cream
　　150ml milk
　　1kg potatoes, peeled and cut into small matchsticks
　　black pepper

Method
1. Preheat the oven to 190°C/375°F/Gas 5.
2. Heat the oil and fry the onion until soft and browned.
3. Add the anchovy fillets and cook to a paste (approximately 5 minutes).
4. Add the cream and milk and bring to the boil, then remove from the heat immediately.
5. Mix with the potatoes, season well and put in a greased ovenproof dish.
6. Cook in the preheated oven for 50 minutes–1 hour until nicely browned on top.

Tip
All the work involved in this dish is in the preparation of the potatoes, so if you can get someone to help here you can halve the preparation time.

Japaneasy Noodles
Serves 2
Prep time: 10 minutes **V**

Ingredients
160g packet yakisoba noodles
1 tablespoon (15ml) oil
1 bunch of spring onions, sliced
2 cloves garlic, crushed
2 teaspoons (10ml) minced chilli
1 teaspoon (5ml) minced ginger
¼ Savoy cabbage, finely shredded

Method
1. Cook the noodles in boiling water for 2 minutes, then drain.
2. Meanwhile, heat the oil and fry the spring onions, garlic, chilli, ginger and cabbage.
3. Add the noodles and sauce sachet to the other ingredients and stir. Serve hot or cold.

Leftovers

Savoy cabbage
West Country Chicken (page 135)
Pot-roasted Chicken (page 143)
Stir-fried Greens (page 182)

Hot 'n' Spicy Noodles
Serves 2
Prep time: 5 minutes **V**

Ingredients
    125g medium egg noodles
    2 tablespoons (30ml) oil
    ½ bunch of spring onions, sliced
    2 cloves garlic, crushed
    1 tablespoon (15ml) minced chilli
    2 tablespoons (30ml) soy sauce

Method
1. Cook the noodles in boiling water for 4 minutes, then drain.
2. Meanwhile, heat 1 tablespoon (15ml) of the oil and quickly stir-fry the spring onions, garlic and chilli.
3. Add the drained noodles, soy sauce and the remaining oil, stir well and serve.

Leftovers

Spring Onions
Bean Salsa (page 21)
Chicken Chow Mein (page 33)
Avocado and Salsa Tortillas (page 39)
Thai Lamb (page 52)
Spaghetti Tunagnese (page 163)

Noodle Salad
Serves 4
Prep time: 5 minutes **V** ✳

Ingredients

For the salad
>225g medium egg noodles
>4 tomatoes, roughly chopped
>1 bunch of spring onions, chopped

For the dressing
>3 tablespoons (45ml) oil
>1 tablespoon (15ml) white wine vinegar
>1 tablespoon (15ml) soy sauce
>1 teaspoon (5ml) Dijon mustard
>1 teaspoon (5ml) honey or sugar

Method
1. Cook the noodles in boiling water for 4 minutes, then plunge them in cold water to stop them cooking and drain well.
2. Mix the noodles with the tomatoes and spring onions.
3. Put the dressing ingredients in a screw-top jar and shake well, then pour over the salad.

Curry-style Couscous
Serves 4
Prep time: 10 minutes **V Ve** ✳

Ingredients
250g couscous
2 tablespoons raisins
2 tablespoons toasted flaked almonds
500ml vegetable stock, made with 1 stock cube and
boiling water

Method
1. Place all the ingredients in a saucepan and bring to the
boil.
2. Remove from the heat and allow to stand for 5 minutes
until the stock is absorbed.
3. Stir before serving.

Tip
This is even nicer if you have some fresh coriander that you
can add to the finished dish.

Tabbouleh (2)
Serves 4
Prep time: 10 minutes + 1 hour soaking **V Ve** ✳

Ingredients
    125g bulgar wheat, soaked in water for 1 hour
    2 tomatoes, chopped
    1 green pepper, deseeded and diced
    ½ cucumber, diced
    1 bunch of coriander, chopped
    4 tablespoons (60ml) oil
    juice of 1 lemon
    salt and black pepper

Method
1. Squeeze out as much water as you can from the bulgar wheat.
2. Mix the bulgar wheat with the tomatoes, green pepper, cucumber and coriander.
3. Put the oil and lemon juice in a screw-top jar and shake well.
4. Mix the dressing with the salad, season and serve.

Pilau Rice
Serves 4
Prep time: 5 minutes + 10 minutes cooking + 10 minutes
standing ✳

Ingredients
2 teaspoons (10ml) oil or butter
1 small onion, chopped
½ teaspoon whole coriander seeds
½ teaspoon whole cardamom pods
½ teaspoon whole cumin seeds
250g basmati rice, soaked
500ml chicken or vegetable stock, made with 1 stock
cube and boiling water

Method
1. Heat the oil or butter and fry the onion until soft and just starting to brown.
2. Add the spices and stir-fry for 30 seconds–1 minute. This is just to get them to release their flavours – be careful not to burn them.
3. Add the rice, stir quickly, then add the stock.
4. Bring to the boil, cover tightly and simmer for 10 minutes until the rice has absorbed the stock.
5. Take off the heat and allow to stand for 10 minutes before stirring up the rice and serving.

Tip
If you forget to soak the rice, at least put it in a sieve and run cold water through it before cooking.

Turkish Pilau
Serves 4
Prep time: 25 minutes **V Ve** ✳

Ingredients
    1 tablespoon (15ml) oil
    3 tablespoons pine nuts
    1 onion, chopped
    250g long-grain rice
    6 whole cardamom seeds
    700ml vegetable stock, made with 1 stock cube and
       boiling water
    salt and black pepper

Method
1. Heat the oil and fry the pine nuts until golden, then remove from the pan and use the oil to fry the onion.
2. Add the rice and cardamom, stir, add the stock and season.
3. Cook for about 15 minutes until the rice is cooked.
4. Stir in the pine nuts before serving.

Egg-fried Rice
Serves 6–8
Prep time: 20 minutes **V**

Ingredients
- 400g basmati rice
- 2 tablespoons (30ml) oil
- 90g frozen peas
- 1 bunch of spring onions, chopped
- 1 tablespoon (15ml) soy sauce
- 2 eggs, beaten

Method
1. Cook the rice in boiling water until tender – about 15 minutes. Rinse in cold water and drain well.
2. Heat the oil and stir-fry the rice, peas and spring onions for 2 minutes.
3. Add the soy sauce and beaten egg and continue to stir-fry until the eggs set.

Leftovers

Eggs
Chinese Omelette Rolls (page 25)
Kidney Bean Kedgeree (page 30)
Toasted Omelette Sandwich (page 46)
Pipérade (page 47)
Huevos Rancheros (page 157)
Omelette (page 161)

Nut and Apricot Dessert
Serves 2
Prep time: 5 minutes **V** ✳

Ingredients
    100g Greek yogurt
    1 tablespoon toasted flaked almonds
    50g ready-to-eat apricots, sliced
    1 tablespoon sunflower seeds
    1 tablespoon (15ml) runny honey

Method
1. Place the yogurt in a dessert bowl and sprinkle with the almonds, apricots and sunflower seeds.
2. Drizzle with the honey and serve immediately.

Tip
You can replace the almonds with toasted pine nuts: toast them on foil under the grill, watching carefully to ensure they don't burn.

Rhubarb Crumble
Serves 4
Prep time: 20 minutes + 50 minutes cooking **V** ✳

Ingredients
>   500g rhubarb
>   1 tablespoon caster sugar
>   juice of 1 large orange

For the crumble
>   75g butter
>   75g plain flour
>   75g + 1 tablespoon demerara sugar
>   75g porridge oats

Method
1. Preheat the oven to 200°C/400°F/Gas 6.
2. Trim the ends off the rhubarb and cut into 3cm pieces.
3. Place the rhubarb, caster sugar and orange juice in an ovenproof dish.
4. Rub together the butter, flour and demerara sugar until you have a mixture resembling breadcrumbs. Stir in the porridge oats and spoon over the rhubarb. Sprinkle with the remaining tablespoon of demerara sugar.
5. Cook, uncovered, in the preheated oven for 45–50 minutes.
6. Leave to stand for 5–10 minutes before serving.

Tip
This is a favourite for a Sunday lunch dessert. Serve with cream, crème fraîche or custard. The crumble topping can be used to cover other seasonal fruit: soft fruit can be used as above but hard fruit should be gently stewed for 5–10 minutes before using.

Eton Mess
Serves 12
Prep time: 10 minutes + 1 hour chilling **V**

Ingredients
750g strawberries, sliced
2 tablespoons caster sugar
12 small meringues, broken
1 litre whipping cream, whipped until thick

Method
1. Mix together the strawberries and sugar and leave to chill for 1 hour to allow the strawberry juices to flow.
2. When ready to make the pudding, mix all the ingredients together and pile into a huge bowl to serve.

Tip
Make this when strawberries are plentiful, not in the middle of winter when only imported expensive ones are available.

Cinnamon Rock Buns
Makes 6
Prep time: 10 minutes + 20 minutes cooking **V** ✳

Ingredients
    200g plain flour
    1 teaspoon ground cinnamon
    100g margarine
    100g + 1 tablespoon demerara sugar
    1 egg, beaten
    2 tablespoons (30ml) milk

Method
1. Preheat the oven to 200°C/400°F/Gas 6.
2. Rub together the flour, cinnamon, margarine and sugar until they resemble breadcrumbs.
3. Stir in the egg and milk.
4. Drop 6 spoonfuls of the mixture on to a baking tray and sprinkle with the remaining tablespoon of demerara sugar.
5. Bake in the preheated oven for 20 minutes until golden brown. These buns are best served while still warm.

Tip
As the buns are made with plain flour they will not rise, but they smell divine while cooking and taste delicious.

Leftovers

Eggs
Kidney Bean Kedgeree (page 30)
Tomato and Herb Omelette (page 32)
Scrambled Curried Eggs with Chapattis (page 42)
Toasted Omelette Sandwich (page 46)
Pipérade (page 47)
Egg and Lentil Curry (page 50)
Huevos Rancheros (page 157)
Omelette (page 161)

Crispy-topped Flapjacks
Makes 12
Prep time: 5 minutes + 25 minutes cooking + 10 minutes standing **V**

Ingredients
150g melted butter
150g + 1 tablespoon demerara sugar
250g porridge oats

Method
1. Preheat the oven to 170°C/325°F/Gas 3.
2. Combine the butter and demerara sugar.
3. Add the oats and mix in really well.
4. Put the mixture in a greased small roasting or baking tin (approximately 11 × 9 inches/28 × 18 cm) and level the surface with the back of a spoon.
5. Sprinkle with the remaining tablespoon of demerara sugar and bake in the preheated oven for 30 minutes.
6. Leave to stand in the tin for 10 minutes before turning out, then cut into squares or fingers to serve.

Index

If you enjoyed this book here is a selection of other bestselling non-fiction titles from Headline

JAMES HERRIOT	Graham Lord	£6.99 ☐
RICHARD BRANSON	Mick Brown	£8.99 ☐
THE GIRL FROM LEAM LANE	Piers Dudgeon	£5.99 ☐
GODS OF EDEN	Andrew Collins	£7.99 ☐
MARYON STEWART'S ZEST FOR LIFE PLAN	Maryon Stewart	£6.99 ☐
SIXTH SENSE	Susie Johns	£7.99 ☐
ADVENTURES IN WONDERLAND	Sheryl Garratt	£7.99 ☐
LOCK, STOCK AND TWO SMOKING BARRELS	Guy Ritchie	£6.99 ☐
SBS	John Parker	£6.99 ☐
ONCE A PILGRIM	Will Scully	£6.99 ☐
FORENSIC FINGERPRINTS	Hugh Miller	£6.99 ☐

Headline books are available at your local bookshop or newsagent. Alternatively, books can be ordered direct from the publisher. Just tick the titles you want and fill in the form below. Prices and availability subject to change without notice.

Buy four books from the selection above and get free postage and packaging and delivery within 48 hours. Just send a cheque or postal order made payable to Bookpoint Ltd to the value of the total cover price of the four books. Alternatively, if you wish to buy fewer than four books the following postage and packaging applies:

UK and BFPO £4.30 for one book; £6.30 for two books; £8.30 for three books.

Overseas and Eire: £4.80 for one book; £7.10 for 2 or 3 books (surface mail)

Please enclose a cheque or postal order made payable to *Bookpoint Limited*, and send to: Headline Publishing Ltd, 39 Milton Park, Abingdon, OXON OX14 4TD, UK.
Email Address: orders@bookpoint.co.uk

If you would prefer to pay by credit card, our call team would be delighted to take your order by telephone. Our direct line 01235 400 414 (lines open 9.00 am–6.00 pm Monday to Saturday 24 hour message answering service). Alternatively you can send a fax on 01235 400 454.

Name ....

Address ....

....

....

If you would prefer to pay by credit card, please complete:
Please debit my Visa/Access/Diner's Card/American Express (delete as applicable) card number:

Signature .... Expiry Date..............